Table of Contents

Practice Test #1 4
  Practice Questions 4
  Answers and Explanations 22
Practice Test #2 33
  Practice Questions 33
  Answers and Explanations 50

Practice Test #1

Practice Questions

1. A norm-referenced assessment would most likely be used to:
    a. determine whether or not a group of students is meeting state-mandated standards
    b. determine whether or not an individual student is meeting state-mandated standards
    c. identify candidates for a gifted education program
    d. diagnose a student with an emotional disability

2. Which of the following types of assessments would most likely be used to measure student progress at the midpoint of an instructional unit and identify areas for reteaching?
    a. Formative assessment
    b. Norm-referenced assessment
    c. Portfolio assessment
    d. Summative assessment

3. Which of the following is an example of a performance assessment?
    a. Students in an art class are assigned a project in which they select a famous painting and create a Cubist version of that painting
    b. Students in a science class are graded on their ability to successfully replicate an experiment
    c. Students in a Spanish class are required to memorize and deliver a Spanish-language monologue to their class
    d. All of the above

4. A teacher is most likely to use a rubric when:
    a. students in the class are at various academic levels
    b. he or she is grading a performance assessment that has multiple components
    c. he or she is teaching students with limited English skills
    d. he or she is assessing students in order to place them into differentiated reading groups

5. Which of the following is an example of effective use of student self-assessment?
    a. Mr. Banks allows his students to grade their own math tests and report the scores to him
    b. Ms. Franco asks her class to trade and grade their social studies tests
    c. Mr. Cameron asks students to complete self-assessment rubrics for their essays, and then holds writing conferences with his students to discuss their essays
    d. Ms. Jackson allows her students to resubmit homework assignments on which they performed poorly

6. Sabrina is a 7th grade student who recently transferred from another school. She completed only 60 percent of the questions on her math diagnostic assessment correctly. Upon closer examination of the items Sabrina missed, her teacher notices that Sabrina demonstrates a high level of mastery of about 60 percent of the concepts covered on the test (including word problems), but has absolutely no understanding of the other 40 percent of the material. Based on this information, the best step for the teacher to take would be to:
   a. refer Sabrina for special education services
   b. transfer Sabrina to a remedial math class
   c. find out if Sabrina has reading difficulties
   d. arrange for Sabrina to receive tutoring in the concept areas she has not yet mastered

7. Mr. Mitchell conducted a formative assessment to measure his students' grasp of a recently taught unit on weather. He was disappointed to find that his students performed poorly. Mr. Mitchell's co-teacher suggested that they reevaluate the validity of the assessment. What does the co-teacher mean by this?
   a. They should check to make sure they graded the test accurately
   b. They should consider whether or not the test directly measures the concepts covered in the unit
   c. They should reassess the quality of their instructional design for this unit
   d. They should consider using a different format for the assessment

8. Mrs. Vargas is designing a multiple choice summative assessment to measure her 6th grade students' understanding of a reading unit. The unit contains 10 learning objectives. Mrs. Vargas wants to ask enough questions to accurately measure her students' comprehension of the unit and minimize the effect of guessing. However, she also wants to minimize the length of the test because of her young students' shorter attention spans. Approximately how many questions for each learning objective should the assessment contain?
   a. 1-3 questions per learning objective
   b. 3-5 questions per learning objective
   c. 5-7 questions per learning objective
   d. 7-10 questions per learning objective

9. Ms. Hamilton is designing an assignment for her 9th grade history class that requires the students to write a research report on a historical figure from the 20th century. Which of the following assignment structures would be most likely to maximize student success and build study skills?
   a. Giving the students a project outline with a due date and requiring the students' parents to sign off on this information
   b. Asking the students to report their chosen topic to the teacher at least one week prior to the due date
   c. Scheduling several "check-in" deadlines by which students must decide on a topic, write an outline, and turn in a rough draft
   d. Allowing students to turn in a rough draft for revision at least two weeks before the project deadline

10. Mr. Shields has several students in his science class who are significantly below grade level in reading. He is concerned that their poor reading skills will hinder their ability to perform well on the written quizzes he has designed. In order to accurately measure these students' understanding of the instructional material, Mr. Shields should:
    a. give these students a less challenging version of the quizzes that the other students are taking
    b. design an alternative assessment for these students that does not require any reading
    c. allow the students who are at very low reading levels to take the quizzes orally
    d. give the students who are at very low reading levels the same test as their peers, but add a few points to their scores to compensate for their low reading levels

11. Sanjay is always enthusiastic and willing to contribute to discussions in Mrs. Williams' U.S. history class. Although his responses convey a general understanding of the subject matter, he tends to offer long and rambling answers that cause other students to quickly lose interest in the discussion. Which of the following techniques would be most helpful to deal with this problem?
    a. After he finishes, Mrs. Williams should summarize Sanjay's comment to draw the other students back into the discussion
    b. Mrs. Williams should interrupt Sanjay after a few seconds and redirect the question to another student
    c. Mrs. Williams should stop calling on Sanjay since he disrupts the flow of the discussion
    d. Mrs. Williams should interrupt Sanjay after a few minutes and ask him to summarize what he has just said

12. Which of the following techniques would be most effective for helping elementary school students prepare for a class discussion?
    a. Giving students a few moments to write out their thoughts before sharing them with the class.
    b. Giving students the questions the day before the discussion so they can prepare their responses as homework.
    c. Giving students a few minutes to discuss their thoughts with a partner before the class discussion.
    d. All of the above.

13. Amanda has leaned over and begun whispering excitedly to her neighbor during Mr. Sanders's biology lesson. In order to address Amanda's distracting behavior without disrupting his lesson, Mr. Sanders should try which of the following strategies FIRST?
    a. Ignore Amanda until she stops since she is probably just trying to get attention
    b. Make eye contact with Amanda to convey his awareness and disapproval of her behavior
    c. Stop the lesson and ask Amanda to be quiet
    d. Drop a Post-it note on Amanda's desk that asks her to leave the room

14. Marcus has just volunteered to answer a question in math class, but his answer is incorrect. Which of the following would be the most effective method to help Marcus and the class arrive at the correct answer without damaging Marcus's confidence?
    a. Telling Marcus that he is wrong and calling on another student who usually has the correct answer
    b. Gently pointing out the error and helping Marcus work through the problem correctly
    c. Working the problem out on the board to ensure there is no confusion
    d. Asking Marcus to come up to the board and work out the problem again so he can discover his error

15. Mrs. Silvio is an ESOL teacher who is putting together a presentation for general education teachers to help them effectively teach ESOL students in their classes. She wants to create a slide that lists the most important considerations that a teacher should weigh when deciding whether to correct a serious grammatical error a student has made while answering a question in front of the class. Which of the following is the biggest risk a teacher takes if he or she corrects an ESOL student in front of the class?
   a. The teacher might distract the class from the lesson by correcting the student
   b. The student might get angry or defensive if he or she is corrected in front of the class
   c. The student might feel embarrassed and refrain from participating in future class discussions
   d. It is impolite to correct grammar in many cultures, so the student might be offended.

16. Which of the following is the most effective method for teachers to convey high expectations for student performance?
   a. Making each student's performance known to the entire class, regardless of whether their performance is high or low
   b. Relying exclusively on standardized test results to evaluate students' performance
   c. Grouping students into classes based on either "high" or "low" academic performance
   d. Developing personal relationships with all students regardless of their current level of academic performance and demonstrating a willingness to help all students equally

17. Proximity control is a classroom management strategy that is best employed:
   a. only when all other techniques to address off-task behavior have been tried
   b. when separating the student from peers has failed to result in improved behavior
   c. when the student is exhibiting exceptionally defiant and offensive behavior
   d. as soon as the teacher notices that a student is off task

18. Active listening involves all of the following EXCEPT:
   a. making eye contact with the speaker
   b. constructively criticizing the speaker
   c. facing the speaker
   d. making statements that demonstrate understanding of what the speaker has said

19. Mr. Tolleson recently had his annual performance review. Although his principal lauded his engaging lessons and classroom management skills, she suggested that his unit planning skills need improvement. Which of the following would be the most important FIRST step for Mr. Tolleson to take to improve his unit planning skills?
   a. Searching the Internet for information on unit planning
   b. Visiting the website of a national education organization to find information
   c. Asking his colleagues how they plan their units
   d. Assessing his current unit planning strategies to determine their strengths and weaknesses

20. Ms. Bingham is a new 5th grade teacher who is experiencing problems with classroom management, and she has asked her mentor teacher for help. The most effective step the mentor teacher could take would be to:
   a. refer Ms. Bingham to the vice principal who is in charge of discipline
   b. offer to observe Ms. Bingham's class and provide suggestions
   c. let Ms. Bingham borrow one of her books on classroom management
   d. tell the other 5th grade teachers that Ms. Bingham is struggling and that they should keep an eye on her

21. Mr. Samuels administered a formative assessment to his 30-student algebra class. He found that about 60 percent of his class failed to master a learning objective necessary to understand the next unit. The most effective strategy for Mr. Samuels to pursue would be to:
    a. move on with the next unit since some students did master the prerequisite objective
    b. reteach the lesson using the same method that he did the first time
    c. consult with other math teachers to deliver a more effective lesson for this learning objective
    d. assign additional homework addressing the learning objective to students who failed to master it

22. All of the following are types of professional development in which teachers should engage consistently EXCEPT:
    a. meeting with students' parents and guardians
    b. participating in mentor-mentee relationships with other teachers
    c. attending school- and district-mandated seminars on teaching strategies and technology use
    d. conducting self-assessments of teaching effectiveness

23. Which of the following activities involves the use of critical thinking skills?
    a. Writing a research paper
    b. Solving a word problem
    c. Categorizing objects
    d. All of the above

24. Critical thinking ability is best assessed using:
    a. authentic assessments
    b. written assessments
    c. oral assessments
    d. criterion-referenced assessments

25. Ms. Sumner has asked her 10th grade civics class to read two legal briefs on a civil rights case and determine which one they find more persuasive. This activity requires students to use which of the following critical thinking skills?
    a. Appraising evidence and evaluating arguments
    b. Communicating with clarity and precision
    c. Recognizing problems and proposing solutions
    d. All of the above

26. Mrs. Baker is an English teacher who has been asked by her principal to explain how she assesses her students' critical thinking ability in writing assignments. Which of the following aspects of writing most clearly reflects a student's ability to think critically?
    a. Use of correct spelling and grammar
    b. Creative content
    c. Logical organization of content
    d. Use of high-level vocabulary

27. Which of the following activities in science class requires the most extensive use of critical thinking skills?
    a. Conducting an experiment by following a sheet of instructions
    b. Memorizing the parts of a cell
    c. Using a telescope to view constellations
    d. Using physics principles to select a material from a list that will make a building earthquake resistant

28. An 8th grade teacher has noticed that her students get off task very quickly when confronted with word problems because they find these types of problems very challenging. Which of the following strategies would be most helpful in addressing this problem?
    a. Allowing students to work in groups to solve the problems
    b. Posting steps for solving problems and checking in with students to remind them to follow the steps
    c. Assigning fewer word problems and more standard math problems
    d. Assigning additional problems to students who are off task

29. A student who is a kinesthetic learner will comprehend concepts best by:
    a. reading and writing about them
    b. listening to the teacher discuss them
    c. engaging in active, hands-on practice with them
    d. discussing them with others

30. According to Howard Gardner's theory of multiple intelligences, which of the following statements is true?
    a. Everyone has only one type of intelligence
    b. Students who don't do well in schools that emphasize linguistic and logical-mathematical intelligence may still be highly intelligent in other domains
    c. Schools often overwhelm students by asking them to activate too many different types of intelligence at once
    d. Students who have high levels of musical, physical, or interpersonal intelligence usually perform poorly in school

31. Students with high levels of interpersonal intelligence will be more successful when they:
    a. work in groups
    b. work independently
    c. have a choice of assignments
    d. are allowed to complete assignments in a series of short intervals with frequent breaks

32. Mr. Townsend has a student in his science class who has been diagnosed with dysgraphia. Which of the following accommodations would be most helpful for this student?
    a. Allowing the student to use a calculator to solve math problems
    b. Allowing the student to sit near the front of the room
    c. Allowing the student to photocopy another student's class notes for his or her use
    d. None of the above

33. A student who suffers from problems with executive functioning will most likely struggle in which of the following areas?
   a. Forming social relationships with peers
   b. Completing assignments on time
   c. Developing motor skills
   d. Learning simple tasks

34. Samantha is a 3rd grade student who still struggles with phonological awareness and blending. Her reading fluency is well below grade level. However, she can explain herself orally using very precise grammar and has an excellent vocabulary. In order to address the challenges that Samantha is facing, her teacher should:
   a. ask Samantha to read aloud in class often so that she can get more practice
   b. send a note to Samantha's parents asking them to have her practice reading at home more often
   c. place Samantha in an ESL class
   d. have Samantha tested for dyslexia and evaluated for special education services in reading

35. Which of the following activities would be most helpful in encouraging students to explore cultural diversity?
   a. Assigning students a project requiring them to research their family backgrounds
   b. Reading about and discussing the contributions of diverse individuals and cultures in class
   c. Watching a movie about the experiences of immigrants in the U.S.
   d. Asking students to write a personal essay describing their family's cultural values and practices

36. According to the *Code of Ethics and Principles of Professional Conduct of the Education Profession in Florida*, which of the following is NOT an obligation of professional educators?
   a. Making a reasonable effort to protect students from conditions harmful to learning
   b. Maintaining the confidentiality of personally identifiable information
   c. Ensuring that students have a safe home environment
   d. Making a reasonable effort to protect students from harassment and discrimination

37. Which of the following actions would constitute a violation of the *Code of Ethics and Principles of Professional Conduct of the Education Profession in Florida*?
   a. Intentionally making false statements about a colleague
   b. Misrepresenting one's professional qualifications
   c. Interfering with a colleague's ability to exercise their political or civil rights
   d. All of the above

38. Tanya is an 11th grade student who has been legally adopted by her aunt and uncle. She is under 18 years of age. The Family Educational Rights and Privacy Act (FERPA) states that a school would need to obtain her guardians' permission to release Tanya's educational records in all of the following situations EXCEPT when:
   a. a local organization is evaluating students for college scholarships and wants Tanya's transcripts
   b. Tanya's mother calls the school to find out how she is performing in her classes
   c. Tanya is transferring to another school and the new school needs her records
   d. the agency that helped with Tanya's adoption requests a copy of her grades

39. Julio is a high school student, and his parents have called the school to express their dissatisfaction with his grade in science. They and Julio believe that he was unfairly penalized for missing a test due to illness, and that this significantly lowered his overall grade for the course. The school has determined that the teacher did penalize Julio in accordance with his own and the school's policies. The school has therefore refused to change Julio's grade. The Family Educational Rights and Privacy Act (FERPA) states that since Julio's parents' request has been denied, Julio's parents are entitled to:
   a. request a formal hearing on the school's decision
   b. insert a note into Julio's file that documents their dispute regarding the grade
   c. request that the teacher be suspended
   d. do none of the above; FERPA does not grant them the right to take any further action

40. Which of the following actions would constitute a violation of the statute of the *Code of Ethics and Principles of Professional Conduct of the Education Profession in Florida* that prohibits giving or receiving gifts in exchange for favors?
   a. Rewarding students who perform well on standardized tests with a pizza party
   b. Giving candy and other small prizes to students who are well-behaved
   c. Helping a neighbor with yard work in exchange for a free laptop computer for the classroom
   d. Taking money from a student's parents in exchange for tutoring that student during the teacher's prep period

41. According to the *Code of Ethics and Principles of Professional Conduct of the Education Profession in Florida*, a licensed educator must report arrests or charges involving possession of a controlled substance or abuse of a child within:
   a. 2 hours
   b. 24 hours
   c. 36 hours
   d. 48 hours

42. The cognitive state of children between the ages of two and six who are at the preoperational stage according to Piaget's Stages of Cognitive Development can be best characterized as:
   a. benevolent
   b. egocentric
   c. abstract
   d. logical

43. According to Piaget's Stages of Cognitive Development, children are best equipped to engage in problem solving and critical thinking at the:
   a. concrete operational stage
   b. preoperational stage
   c. formal operational stage
   d. sensorimotor stage

44. Which of the following tasks would be most appropriate for a child at the concrete operational stage of cognitive development?
   a. Grouping objects into categories by shape and color
   b. Solving a word problem using algebra
   c. Identifying the main idea of a story
   d. Grasping and stacking blocks

45. Which of the following strategies would be most likely to encourage students' intrinsic motivation to learn?
    a. Designing lessons that incorporate students' personal experiences and interests
    b. Providing positive reinforcement for students' effort, as well as for achievement
    c. Offering prizes such as candy and free time to the highest-performing students
    d. Posting the work of high-performing students in a public place in the classroom as an example

46. Amelia is a 4th grade student who has been diagnosed with a mild hearing impairment. Which of the adaptations listed below would be most effective for Amelia's teacher to adopt?
    a. Ensuring that lessons are delivered in a loud and clear voice, and reviewing the main points of the lesson with Amelia afterward to ensure she heard and understood them
    b. Referring Amelia for special education services since she cannot succeed in a mainstream classroom
    c. Standing very close to Amelia during instruction and speaking very loudly
    d. Learning sign language and using it to communicate with Amelia

47. Caleb demonstrates a high level of academic aptitude, but he is frequently distracted in class and behaves impulsively. He also has extreme difficulty concentrating on tasks and planning ahead. As a result, Caleb's academic performance is below average and he often becomes frustrated with tasks that take more than a few minutes. Which of the following statements about Caleb is most likely true?
    a. Caleb's poor academic performance is caused by parental neglect
    b. Caleb's academic performance could be improved if he were given more challenging assignments
    c. Caleb exhibits strong executive functioning skills, but he is probably suffering from an emotional disability
    d. Despite his strong academic aptitude, Caleb is performing poorly in school because he has low executive functioning skills

48. Which of the following statements do NOT typically describe students with emotional disabilities?
    a. They may exhibit inappropriate social behaviors
    b. They experience frequent episodes of anxiety and depression
    c. Their emotional disability may cause them to struggle academically
    d. They have unusually high self-esteem

49. Which of the following teacher behaviors demonstrates application of the principles of mastery learning?
    a. Grading student work on a "curve"
    b. Allowing all students to pursue independent study and conduct self-assessments of their progress, regardless of their current academic levels
    c. Requiring students to demonstrate competence in prerequisite skills before allowing them to proceed to subsequent lessons
    d. Dividing students into groups based on academic performance and assigning them more or less challenging assignments accordingly

50. According to Bloom's taxonomy of cognitive skills, which of the following activities requires the highest-order cognitive thinking skills?
    a. Memorizing a list of foreign-language words and their English equivalents
    b. Creating an invention for the school science fair
    c. Applying a newly-learned geometry formula to solve a story problem
    d. Reading and understanding the contents of an academic paper

51. Which of the following is the most effective way to incorporate a variety of learning styles into instruction?
    a. Allowing students to choose their own form of assessment
    b. Including visual aids and hands-on practice during verbal instruction
    c. Incorporating technology into instruction and assignments
    d. Inserting stretch breaks into lessons

52. An anticipatory set is used by teachers to:
    a. provide additional practice for students who have not yet mastered a learning objective
    b. focus students on the upcoming lesson and tap into prerequisite knowledge
    c. teach prerequisite skills
    d. do none of the above

53. According to Madeline Hunter's "Instructional Theory into Practice" teaching model, which of the following is the best example of guided practice?
    a. Students complete an assignment in pairs
    b. A teacher works one-on-one with a student to help him or her complete an assignment
    c. Students practice a skill they have just learned and receive immediate feedback from their instructor
    d. The teacher completes problems on the board while the students take notes

54. During a math lesson, a teacher conducts a check for understanding and discovers that only about half of the class understands the lesson. The FIRST step the teacher should take to correct this problem should be to:
    a. proceed with the lesson as planned and follow up with the students who were confused afterwards
    b. start the lesson over from the beginning
    c. continue with the lesson, but plan to revamp it and reteach it the following day
    d. immediately take steps to identify and resolve the source of confusion, and then conduct a follow-up check for understanding to assess the effectiveness of these steps

55. Which of the following is the best example of a specific, measurable learning objective?
    a. The student will be able to identify the parts of a cell
    b. The student will understand the causes of the Civil War
    c. Students will know about electricity
    d. Students will learn about the Great Depression

56. A teacher has chosen the following as a learning objective for her anatomy class: "Students will be able to earn a score of 90 percent or above on a test about the circulatory system." Which of the following statements best describes the major weakness of this learning objective?
    a. The learning objective is not specific enough
    b. The learning objective is not measurable
    c. The learning objective is not realistic
    d. There is no distinction between the learning objective and the method used to assess it

57. Which of the following is a skill associated with print awareness?
    a. Understanding that when someone is reading a text aloud, what they say is derived from the text on the page
    b. Knowing how to spell
    c. Being able to sound out printed words
    d. Being able to comprehend printed words

58. When a student is able to orally break words such as "she" down into their component sounds, this is evidence of:
    a. understanding of phonics
    b. print awareness
    c. phonemic awareness
    d. none of the above

59. A student who grasps the alphabetic principle:
    a. can decode any word if given enough time
    b. will be able to read fluently
    c. can be expected to comprehend most written instructions
    d. understands that letters and combinations of letters correspond to spoken sounds

60. A words correct per minute screening test is used primarily to:
    a. identify students who have weak reading fluency skills
    b. assess the breadth of students' vocabulary
    c. assess students' reading comprehension skills
    d. identify students who have poor phonemic awareness

61. Mr. Callahan is preparing to have his students read a novel, and he wants to ensure they have the necessary vocabulary to understand the plot. The best approach for addressing this concern would be to:
    a. ensure that students have dictionaries available while they're reading
    b. read the novel aloud and address any new vocabulary words as they arise
    c. teach and practice new vocabulary words and concepts prior to beginning the novel
    d. review the procedures for deducing the meaning of new words using context

62. Ms. Julliard is a 9th grade social studies teacher who is planning a unit on World War II. However, she has many students in her class who are either reading very far above grade level or significantly below grade level. Which of the following approaches would be most appropriate for a class with students who have such diverse ability levels?
   a. Introducing the subject matter in a class lecture and exempting the students with very low reading levels from completing the more challenging reading assignments
   b. Organizing a mandatory after-school reading group so that she can help the low readers with the reading assignments for the unit
   c. Enlisting the students who are higher-level readers to tutor the students who are lower-level readers
   d. Assigning students at each reading level different texts that match their skill levels

63. In order to develop students' reading fluency, teachers should incorporate which of the following activities into their lessons?
   a. Vocabulary building exercises
   b. Extensive practice reading aloud
   c. Extended periods of silent reading
   d. Pop quizzes on reading material

64. The primary purpose of informal reading inventories such as the BRI, CRI-CFC, QRI-4, and ARI is to:
   a. determine whether or not students meet state grade level standards
   b. conduct preliminary diagnostic screening to help determine students' instructional needs
   c. estimate how students will perform on norm-referenced standardized tests
   d. assign grades and assess students' comprehension of individual lessons and units

65. In order for consequences to be effective in managing behavior, they must be:
   a. uniformly negative
   b. uniformly positive
   c. consistently and fairly applied
   d. sufficiently severe to act as a deterrent

66. Which of the following is the most effective procedure for encouraging students' adherence to classroom rules?
   a. Introducing the rules at the beginning of the school year, reviewing them periodically, and citing them when applying consequences
   b. Developing a complex list of potential negative behaviors and their consequences, and requiring students and their parents to sign a copy
   c. Allowing students to decide on and enforce classroom rules democratically
   d. Passing out a copy of the classroom rules and procedures and requiring students to keep it with them at all times

67. Which of the following is the most important consideration when designing a seating chart?
   a. Students like and feel comfortable with the students sitting near them
   b. Students can easily turn their desks to work in groups
   c. The teacher can easily monitor all of the students during instruction and from his or her desk
   d. The teacher's desk is in a convenient location near the instructional focal point of the room

68. Refer to the classroom rules listed below:
   Classroom Rules
   1. Don't hit, kick, or push other students.
   2. Don't chew gum.
   3. Don't curse or insult other students.
   4. Don't talk while the teacher is talking.

Which of the following statements best describes the major flaw in this set of rules?
   a. The rules are too general
   b. The rules focus on prohibiting negative behaviors, and do not state expected positive behaviors
   c. They are too harsh and severe
   d. There are too few rules

69. Which of the following would be effective if included as part of a set of classroom rules?
   a. Students should come to class prepared
   b. Students should practice active listening when others are talking
   c. Students should raise their hand to speak or ask a question during instruction
   d. All of the above

70. Which of the following is NOT an effective way to deal with a student who has repeatedly broken classroom rules?
   a. Moving that student to a desk away from other students
   b. Sending that student to a "time out" in another classroom
   c. Insulting or demeaning the student
   d. Creating a behavior contract with the student

71. Parents should be informed about students' behavior:
   a. only when it is negative
   b. as soon as a pattern of problem behavior emerges
   c. every time a student breaks a classroom rule
   d. only at parent teacher conferences

72. In order to ensure that students follow classroom procedures, the teacher should:
   a. minimize the number and complexity of procedures as much as possible
   b. give students written instructions for all procedures
   c. apply severe consequences when students forget procedures
   d. review and rehearse procedures intensively at the beginning of the school year and periodically throughout the year

73. Which of the following procedures should be taught to students at the beginning of the school year?
   a. Passing papers forward
   b. Sharpening a pencil
   c. What to do when seatwork is finished
   d. All of the above

74. The major benefit of allowing students to participate in the development of classroom rules is that:
    a. it is a fun activity that helps students feel comfortable in the classroom
    b. it makes it easier for students to remember the rules
    c. students are more likely to value and adhere to rules they helped create
    d. this activity teaches students about democratic processes

75. The most important goal in arranging the physical layout of a classroom is:
    a. ensuring that the colors of displays are well-coordinated and relevant to lessons
    b. leaving space open to display student work
    c. ensuring the layout of the room promotes student safety and effective monitoring by the teacher
    d. ensuring that the teacher can move easily around the room during lessons

76. Which of the following statements is true of a behavior contract?
    a. It must involve the student's parents
    b. It should clearly state what behavior is desired and what positive and negative consequences will be applied should the student choose to exhibit or not exhibit the agreed-upon behavior
    c. The most important part of implementing a behavior contract is the discussion and meeting with the student, and follow-up is not always necessary
    d. It is not helpful for the student to participate in the development of the contract

77. The most important FIRST step in delivering differentiated reading instruction is to:
    a. select materials for different reading levels
    b. design differentiated assessments appropriate for students at varied reading levels
    c. assess students to determine the range of reading levels that need to be targeted
    d. place students in reading groups based on their overall academic performance

78. The most important resource for unit and lesson planning is:
    a. student textbooks
    b. the students' own interests
    c. Internet resources and academic journal articles
    d. state and district instructional standards

79. When designing a lesson for a given class period, which of the following steps should be completed FIRST?
    a. Selecting the reading or stimulus material that the students will use
    b. Choosing an assessment method for the material to be learned
    c. Determining what the learning objective for the class period will be
    d. Considering what instructional materials are available

80. Task analysis can be a helpful technique when planning lessons for which of the following learning objectives?
    a. The student will be able to solve a two-step algebraic equation
    b. The student will be able to tie his or her shoes
    c. The student will be able to find the main idea of a news article
    d. All of the above

81. Mrs. Frances is teaching her middle school math class how to find the area of a triangle. Which of the following is the best example of a "check for understanding" that Mrs. Frances could conduct to ensure her students understand the material?
   a. She can give an assessment at the end of the lesson in the form of a pop quiz
   b. She can call on individual students to answer questions during the lesson
   c. She can ask the entire class to indicate their level of understanding at critical points during the lesson using hand signals
   d. She can give students a formative assessment of the material before the lesson begins

82. Which of the following is the most important consideration for unit planning?
   a. Ensuring the unit has a fun and engaging theme
   b. Ensuring the learning objectives within the unit is logically sequenced so that prerequisite skills are taught first
   c. Ensuring students' interests and experiences are incorporated into the unit's theme
   d. Ensuring critical thinking skills are integrated into the unit

83. Mr. Bartlett has designed a science unit that he plans to teach over the next two weeks. On the first day of the unit he discovers that most of the students in his class are missing a critical math skill that is a prerequisite for the unit. How can Mr. Bartlett avoid similar problems in the future?
   a. He can ask the math teacher for a copy of her lesson plans so he knows what she is teaching
   b. He can avoid planning lessons that integrate other subjects
   c. He can conduct a diagnostic assessment of students' prerequisite skills before planning future units
   d. All of the above would be appropriate strategies

84. Teachers are involved in which of the following activities for at-risk students?
   a. Implementing pre-referral interventions
   b. Creating Individualized Education Plans (IEPs)
   c. Implementing IEPs and evaluating their effectiveness
   d. All of the above

85. Mr. Jones has strong suspicions that a student is being physically abused at home. The student has not confirmed that abuse has occurred, but the student's physical condition suggests that this is the case. How should the teacher proceed?
   a. He should contact the appropriate authorities immediately
   b. He should not take any action unless the student admits that abuse has occurred
   c. He should not say anything since it is not his business
   d. He should schedule a conference with the parents to confront them

86. Which of the following is a general education classroom teacher's responsibility during the IEP creation process?
   a. Convening the IEP conference
   b. Attending the IEP conference
   c. Writing the IEP
   d. Getting the student's parents to approve the IEP

87. Which of the following statements about Section 504 of the Americans with Disabilities Act and the Individuals with Disabilities Education Act (IDEA) is correct?
 a. Students who qualify for Section 504 protection always qualify for protection under IDEA
 b. Both IDEA and Section 504 only provide protection for students who have a disability that interferes with their learning
 c. IDEA contains procedural safeguards for students with disabilities that interfere with their learning, while Section 504 is designed to protect all disabled individuals from discrimination
 d. Both students who qualify for protection under IDEA and those who qualify for protection under Section 504 must receive Individualized Education Plans (IEPs)

88. According to the Individuals with Disabilities Education Act (IDEA), students who are diagnosed with learning disabilities must be placed in the:
 a. least restrictive environment possible
 b. safest environment possible
 c. environment in which they will be least disruptive
 d. most beneficial environment possible

89. Which of the following statements is true of Florida's mandatory reporting law?
 a. Only obvious abuse must be reported
 b. Reporting of neglect is optional
 c. Suspected child abandonment does not need to be reported
 d. Educators are required to report suspected abuse, neglect, and abandonment

90. When teaching students to use Internet search engines for research, it is most important for the teacher to design a lesson that covers:
 a. how to use search operators such as site: and loc:
 b. how to distinguish reliable, authoritative websites from unreliable ones
 c. how to download and use antivirus software
 d. how to build websites

91. When determining the quality of a webpage for research purposes, students should look for which of the following characteristics?
 a. The page has a low proportion of ads to information and the overall appearance is organized and professional
 b. There is evidence that the site is regularly updated and that the information it contains is up-to-date
 c. The author of the page is identified and is a reliable authority on the research topic
 d. All of the above

92. Mr. Adams is requiring his students to give class presentations on a scientific discovery of their choice. Which of the following software products would be most appropriate for such presentations?
 a. Adobe Acrobat
 b. Microsoft Office
 c. Microsoft PowerPoint
 d. Microsoft Excel

93. When planning lessons, a teacher who incorporates John Dewey's progressive theory of education would be most likely to:
    a. teach students who are struggling separately from the rest of the class
    b. encourage problem solving and real-life experience as paths to learning
    c. provide material rewards for excellent academic performance
    d. encourage competition among students as a means of motivation

94. Maricela is an ESOL student who has recently moved to the U.S. She has shown marked progress in her acquisition of spoken English, grammar, and spelling. However, she still struggles to comprehend English texts at her grade level. What is the most likely cause of the gap between Maricela's ability to read and her comprehension of what she reads?
    a. Maricela has a disability in reading comprehension
    b. Maricela's parents do not speak English to her at home
    c. Maricela lacks the cultural background knowledge and vocabulary to comprehend these texts
    d. Maricela did not receive adequate reading comprehension instruction in her home country

95. Which of the following statements is true of most ESOL students?
    a. The range of intelligence among ESOL students is similar to that among native English-speaking students
    b. ESOL students may need to be placed in special education classes until their English improves
    c. ESOL students mainly struggle in English and reading classes, but their limited English skills do not typically affect their performance in other subject areas
    d. ESOL students should be encouraged to speak only English at home with their parents, even if their parents do not speak English fluently

96. Jarithza is a 4th grade student who moved to the U.S. and enrolled in school about a year ago. English is a second language for her and her family. Although tests conducted in her native language confirm that Jarithza does not have any learning disabilities, she is struggling to perform at grade level in math, reading, and writing. Which of the following strategies is likely to be most effective in improving Jarithza's academic performance?
    a. Ask Jarithza's parents to speak only English at home
    b. Request her parents' permission to place her in special education classes
    c. Lower academic expectations for Jarithza so that she and her parents do not realize she is struggling
    d. Adapt certain aspects of the class to meet Jarithza's needs

97. In order to meet the needs of ESOL students in mainstream classes, teachers should:
    a. incorporate elements related to ESOL students' interests and backgrounds into the curriculum so that they feel valued and accepted
    b. never openly acknowledge any differences between ESOL students and students who are native English speakers
    c. hold ESOL students to lower academic standards than other students
    d. sacrifice the academic needs of students who are proficient in English in order to focus on ESOL students

98. When teaching students in the mainstream classroom who have non-existent or extremely limited English skills, it is most important to:
   a. take steps to build their English vocabulary as much and as quickly as possible
   b. deliver intensive lessons on proper grammar
   c. help their parents find local organizations that teach English
   d. assign another student to tutor them in English

99. Mr. Vale has noticed that the parents of many of his ESOL students do not attend parent teacher conferences because they are embarrassed by their limited English skills. Unfortunately, the school lacks the funds to hire professional translators for conferences. What can Mr. Vale do to alleviate this problem?
   a. Invite bilingual students to volunteer as translators
   b. Look for bilingual community members who are willing to serve as translators with parental consent
   c. Schedule conferences at local restaurants or students' homes so that parents will feel comfortable
   d. Allow students to translate at their own conferences

100. Which of the following students is most likely NOT eligible for special education services?
   a. Juanita, an ESOL student who has not been diagnosed with any learning disabilities but struggles academically
   b. Victor, who has a cognitive impairment caused by a mild brain injury
   c. Sylvia, who has been diagnosed with ADHD
   d. All of these students would be eligible for special education services

Answers and Explanations

1. **C**: Norm-referenced tests are scored on a scale that shows where each student stands in relation to the larger group of test takers, which makes them a useful way to identify candidates for a gifted education program. Unlike criterion-referenced tests, which measure individual students' competency with regard to measurable performance standards, norm-referenced tests are not typically used to determine whether or not students meet state standards, or to diagnose emotional disabilities.

2. **A**: A formative assessment would most likely be used to track student progress over the course of a unit and identify areas for reteaching. Norm-referenced assessments are used to identify high, medium, and low achievers by assessing particular skills and academic areas. Summative assessments are carried out at the end of units to aid learning, and portfolio assessments are designed to emphasize improvement over time.

3. **D**: Creating paintings, replicating experiments, and delivering monologues in foreign languages are all examples of performance assessments. Performance assessments measure students' ability to perform skills they have been taught in class through lectures, demonstrations, readings, and other methods.

4. **B**: A teacher is most likely to use a rubric when he or she is grading a performance assessment that has multiple components. Rubrics allow educators to break a student's performance into different categories and assess each category individually. For instance, a teacher might grade a student's research report using a rubric with three different components: research, organization, and grammar.

5. **C**: Asking students to complete a self-assessment rubric for their essays and then holding writing conferences with each individual student to discuss their assessments is an example of effective use of student self-assessment. Self-assessments allow students to gain a deeper understanding of what quality work looks like, and to more deeply analyze the strengths and weaknesses of their own academic performance.

6. **D**: The teacher should arrange for Sabrina to receive tutoring in the concept areas she has not yet mastered. The information presented suggests that Sabrina's poor performance on the diagnostic test is the result of a gap between the material covered at her current school and that covered at her previous school. Given her strong performance on certain concepts covered by the test, it would be inappropriate to refer her for special education services or transfer her to a remedial class. Since she was able to perform well on problems that require reading, it also appears that poor reading skills are not the issue.

7. **B**: Mr. Mitchell's co-teacher means that they should consider whether or not the test directly measures the concepts covered in the weather unit. It is possible that the students have mastered the learning objectives. However, the assessment questions may contain additional objectives that were not covered.

8. B: In order to accurately assess students' comprehension of the learning objectives and minimize the effect of guessing, Mrs. Vargas should ask at least three questions per objective. However, if she wants her students to maintain appropriate levels of concentration and motivation throughout the test, she should ask no more than five questions per objective.

9. C: By scheduling several "check-in" deadlines by which students must decide on a topic, write an outline, and turn in a rough draft, Ms. Hamilton will facilitate students' understanding of the steps that must be completed to write a research project, and will also increase the chances that students will produce high-quality finished products.

10. C: In order to accurately measure understanding of instructional material, Mr. Shields should allow the students who are at very low reading levels to take the quizzes orally. This method will ensure that these students are held to the same science standards as their peers. It will also ensure that their poor reading ability will not hinder their performance in the class.

11. A: The most appropriate way to deal with this situation would be to summarize Sanjay's comment to draw the other students back into the discussion after he finishes. This method maintains the flow of the discussion without embarrassing the student in question. It would also be appropriate to have a private discussion with the student and ask him to try to be more succinct.

12. C: For elementary students, the most appropriate technique would be to give the students a few minutes to discuss their thoughts with a partner before the class discussion (sometimes called "think-pair-share"). This technique allows students to organize their thoughts and build confidence in the value of their ideas before sharing them with a larger group. Writing assignments and extended homework assignments are challenging tasks for elementary students, and would not be effective methods to prepare students for a class discussion.

13. B: The nonverbal strategy Mr. Sanders should try first to address Amanda's distracting behavior would be to make eye contact with Amanda to convey his awareness and disapproval of her behavior. Asking Amanda to leave the room is an extreme reaction, while ignoring the unacceptable behavior will only encourage it. Making eye contact with Amanda is an effective first step in addressing the problem.

14. B: The most effective method to help Marcus and the class arrive at the correct answer without damaging Marcus's confidence would be to gently point out the error and help Marcus work through the problem correctly. This method would allow Marcus to redeem himself by arriving at the correct answer, and would also ensure that the other students in the class know the correct answer and are not confused.

15. C: The most important argument against correcting the ESOL student is that the student might feel embarrassed and refrain from participating in class discussions in the future if corrected in front of the class. Teachers must weigh this consideration against the possibility that the student will continue to make the error because he or she thinks it is correct.

16. D: One of the most effective methods for teachers to convey high expectations for student performance is to develop personal relationships with all students regardless of their current level of academic performance. Teachers should also demonstrate a willingness to help all students equally. When teachers model the belief that all students make valuable contributions to the classroom community, students can internalize the teacher's confidence in their abilities.

17. D: Proximity control is a classroom management strategy that is best employed as soon as the teacher notices that off-task behavior is occurring. Proximity control, which involves moving close to a student to make that student more aware of the teacher's supervision, is most effective when it is employed immediately. If students' misbehavior has been ignored for an extended period of time or has escalated to a severe stage, they will probably not respond to this technique.

18. B: Although constructive criticism can indicate understanding of what the speaker has said, it is not a necessary component of active listening. Active listening involves giving one's complete attention to the speaker and demonstrating that attention with one's body language and responses.

19. D: The most important first step for Mr. Tolleson to take to improve his unit planning skills would be to assess his current unit planning strategy to determine its strengths and weaknesses. While asking colleagues about their strategies and searching the Internet for information are also helpful approaches, self-assessment is a critical first step for teachers who are attempting to improve their practice.

20. B: The most effective step the mentor teacher could take would be to offer to observe Ms. Bingham's class and provide suggestions. This would allow the mentor teacher to identify specific strengths and weaknesses in Ms. Bingham's approach and offer effective suggestions that she could put into practice right away. Telling other teachers about the problem would be an unprofessional violation of the confidentiality that should exist between a mentor and mentee.

21. C: The most effective strategy for Mr. Samuels to pursue would be to consult with other math teachers to find and deliver a more effective lesson for this learning objective. If more than half of the class did not master the objective, this suggests that Mr. Samuels should reevaluate his instructional strategy for this learning concept and try to teach the concept again using a different approach.

22. A: Teachers should engage in all of these activities consistently, but meeting with students' parents and guardians is a community outreach activity as opposed to a professional development one. Professional development activities such as attending training, collaborating with peers, and engaging in self-assessment are all pursuits that help teachers improve their professional practice through reflection and learning. Conferencing with students' parents and guardians is an aspect of professional practice that can be improved through development activities.

23. D: Writing a research paper, solving a word problem, and categorizing objects are all activities that require students to use critical thinking skills. Critical thinking involves solving problems by identifying them, gathering information, and weighing possible solutions. Critical thinking is used to accomplish complex tasks that require the participant to formulate a plan as opposed to applying a memorized formula.

24. A: Critical thinking ability is best measured using authentic assessments. Since a student's ability to solve problems is a reflection of critical thinking ability, it is crucial that critical thinking skills be tested with authentic problems for which the student has not already been given a solution. For instance, solving a math problem when the teacher has just modeled how to solve that type of problem several times does not require critical thinking skills. Instead, students are simply applying a rote formula. However, solving a word problem that does not directly state what needs to be calculated does require critical thinking skills.

25. A: Ms. Sumner has asked her students to read two legal briefs on a civil rights case and determine which one they find more persuasive. This activity primarily requires students to appraise the evidence and evaluate the arguments presented in the briefs. It does not require communication or problem-solving skills.

26. C: The aspect of writing that most clearly reflects a student's ability to think critically is their ability to logically and effectively organize content to present a coherent argument or exposition on a given topic. This task requires students to categorize information based on factors such as relevance and chronology.

27. D: Solving a physics problem in which students must determine which of several materials will make a building least susceptible to earthquakes requires the most extensive use of students' critical thinking skills. The reason for this is that the activity asks students to formulate a strategy to solve a problem. The other tasks mentioned simply involve following instructions or memorizing information. These activities do not involve extensive use of critical thinking skills.

28. B: The most helpful strategy for addressing this problem would be to post the steps for solving problems in a prominent location. The teacher should also constantly check in with students to remind them to follow the steps and see where they are in the problem-solving process. Students often get off task when they feel overwhelmed by the difficulty of an assignment, but "chunking" the assignment into smaller steps (identify the problem, develop a strategy, etc.) makes the task less daunting and also teaches important critical thinking skills.

29. C: A student who is a kinesthetic learner will comprehend concepts best by engaging in active, hands-on practice. Auditory learners learn best by listening, and visual learners comprehend concepts by watching the teacher model tasks and looking at visual aids.

30. B: According to Howard Gardner's theory of multiple intelligences, students who don't do well in schools that emphasize linguistic and logical-mathematical intelligence may still be highly intelligent in other domains. Gardner theorizes that there are eight domains of intelligence, many of which are not emphasized in traditional educational environments. As a result, students who are highly intelligent in these areas may be mistakenly classified as underachievers.

31. A: Students with high levels of interpersonal intelligence may benefit most from working in groups. This is because they are adept at and enjoy interacting with others. In contrast, students with low levels of interpersonal intelligence may perform poorly when asked to work in groups because their social skills are not as well-developed.

32. C: The most helpful accommodation for a student with dysgraphia would be to allow the student to photocopy another student's class notes for his or her own use. Dysgraphia is a learning disability that causes difficulty forming letters and writing information down in an organized fashion. Although a student may listen to and understand the teacher's science lectures, his or her learning disability may make it difficult for him or her to take organized notes. This reduces the chances that the student will be successful in class. A student with this disability could benefit immensely from being permitted to photocopy another student's notes.

33. B: A student who suffers from problems with executive functioning will most likely struggle with completing assignments on time. Executive functioning disabilities such as ADHD make it difficult for individuals to concentrate on tasks for a prolonged period of time. Students with such

disabilities may need to be seated away from other students to avoid distractions, and they may need to complete assignments in intervals with short activity breaks in between.

34. D: In order to address the challenges that Samantha is facing, her teacher should have Samantha tested for dyslexia and evaluated for special education services in reading. A student who is orally fluent but still has marked difficulties with reading fluency in 3rd grade may have a learning disability, and should therefore be evaluated.

35. B: Reading about and discussing the contributions of diverse individuals and cultures in class would be most helpful in encouraging students to explore cultural diversity. This activity allows students to learn about and discuss cultures other than their own as opposed to actively or passively reflecting on their own experiences.

36. C: Ensuring that students have a safe home environment is not an obligation of professional educators. However, educators are required by state and federal law to report suspected neglect, abuse, or abandonment to the proper authorities.

37. D: Intentionally making false statements about a colleague, misrepresenting one's professional qualifications, and interfering with a colleague's ability to exercise their political or civil rights all constitute violations of the *Code of Ethics and Principles of Professional Conduct of the Education Profession in Florida*.

38. C: The Family Educational Rights and Privacy Act (FERPA) states that a school would need to obtain Tanya's guardians' permission to release her educational records to her mother (who is not her legal guardian) or to outside organizations. However, Tanya's school would not need permission to send Tanya's records to her new school.

39. A: The Family Educational Rights and Privacy Act (FERPA) states that since Julio's parents' initial request was denied, they have the right to a formal hearing. If the hearing does not result in a decision by the school to amend the record, then Julio's parents would be entitled to insert a note into Julio's file that documents their dispute regarding the grade.

40. D: Taking money from a student's parents in exchange for tutoring that student during the teacher's prep period would constitute a violation of the statute of the *Code of Ethics and Principles of Professional Conduct of the Education Profession in Florida* that prohibits giving or receiving gifts in exchange for favors. In this case, the gift is causing the teacher to pay undue attention to a particular student rather than helping students as equitably as possible.

41. D: According to the *Code of Ethics and Principles of Professional Conduct of the Education Profession in Florida*, a licensed educator must report arrests or charges involving possession of a controlled substance or abuse of a child within 48 hours. In addition, teachers must "self-report any conviction, finding of guilt, withholding of adjudication, commitment to a pretrial diversion program, or entering of a plea of guilty or Nolo Contendre for any criminal offense other than a minor traffic violation within forty-eight (48) hours after the final judgment."

42. B: The cognitive state of children between the ages of two and six who are at the preoperational stage according to Piaget's Stages of Cognitive Development can be best characterized as egocentric. Children at this stage of cognitive development are not typically capable of the type of abstract thought required to truly understand and consider another person's point of view.

43. C: According to Piaget's Stages of Cognitive Development, children are best equipped to engage in problem solving and critical thinking at the formal operational stage. This stage begins around age 12, and is marked by the emergence of abstract logic.

44. C: Identifying the main idea of a story would be most appropriate for a child at the concrete operational stage of cognitive development. Children at this stage are developing the capability of induction (generalizing from a specific instance), but have not yet developed the capacity for deductive logic that is required for abstract thinking.

45. A: Designing lessons that incorporate students' personal experiences and interests would be most likely to encourage students' intrinsic motivation to learn. Intrinsic motivation stems from a personal desire to acquire knowledge for its own sake rather than as a means to external rewards such as status or prizes.

46. A: The most effective adaptation for Amelia would be to ensure that lessons are delivered in a loud and clear voice. The teacher should also review the main points of the lesson with Amelia afterward to ensure that she heard and understood them. Standing close to the student throughout instruction would not only interfere with instructional delivery, but would also draw unwanted attention to the student's disability.

47. D: Despite Caleb's strong academic aptitude, he is probably performing poorly in school because he suffers from poor executive functioning skills. These skills enable people to plan ahead and control their impulses, and students with poor executive functioning skills often have difficulty concentrating on and completing complex tasks.

48. D: Students with emotional disabilities may exhibit inappropriate behaviors in social settings, experience academic difficulties, and struggle with anxiety and depression that impede their normal academic and social functioning. Although a small minority of students with emotional disabilities may exhibit high self-esteem, the vast majority of such students experience social rejection and have low self-esteem.

49. C: Requiring students to demonstrate competence in prerequisite skills before allowing them to proceed to subsequent lessons is one of the fundamental principles of mastery learning. Proponents of this approach argue that the vast majority of students can grasp all academic concepts taught if they are given sufficient time and quality instruction.

50. B: According to Bloom's taxonomy of cognitive skills, creating an invention for the school science fair requires the highest-order cognitive activity because it involves synthesis, evaluation, and creation. According to Bloom's original taxonomy, evaluation is the highest-level cognitive task, followed by synthesis. In the revised taxonomy by Anderson, creation is the highest-level task, followed by evaluation.

51. B: Including visual aids and hands-on practice during verbal instruction will expand the appeal of a lesson to visual and kinesthetic learners, as well as auditory learners. While technology can *help* teachers appeal to students with a variety of different learning styles, simply incorporating technology will not necessarily be enough.

52. B: An anticipatory set is used to focus students on the upcoming lesson and tap into prerequisite knowledge. Anticipatory sets can take the form of brief writing assignments or activities that mentally prepare students for the upcoming lesson by activating relevant prior knowledge.

53. C: According to Madeline Hunter's Instructional Theory into Practice teaching model, an example of guided practice would be students practicing a skill they just learned and receiving immediate feedback from their instructor. Guided practice occurs immediately after direct instruction (when the teacher introduces the learning objective) and checks for understanding (when the teacher interacts with students to informally confirm they understand the new material).

54. D: The first step the teacher should take to correct this problem should be to identify and resolve the source of confusion by asking probing questions and attempting to identify and reactivate prerequisite knowledge that some students may have forgotten. After taking these steps and addressing the source of confusion, the teacher should conduct a follow-up check for understanding to assess the effectiveness of these steps. This process will give the teacher more information about what is causing students' confusion, and will help the teacher determine how to proceed.

55. A: "The student will be able to identify the parts of a cell" is an example of a learning objective that is both specific in terms of the task that the student is expected to be able to perform and measurable in the sense that the teacher can concretely observe the extent to which the student is able to perform the task.

56. D: The major weakness of this learning objective is that there is no distinction between the learning objective and the method used to assess it. Learning objectives should state the skill or concept that students are expected to master, and the assessment method should be determined based upon this objective.

57. A: Understanding that when someone is reading a text aloud, what they say is based on the print on the page is a skill associated with print awareness. Print awareness is the understanding that print represents spoken language, and that printed letters are organized in certain ways to serve certain purposes.

58. C: When a student is able to break words such as "she" down into their component sounds, this is evidence of phonemic awareness. Phonemic awareness is a prerequisite skill for phonics. Phonemic awareness involves being able to distinguish the sounds that compose a word, while phonics involves associating those sounds with letters of the alphabet.

59. D: A student who grasps the alphabetic principle understands that letters and combinations of letters correspond to spoken sounds. The alphabetic principle and phonemic awareness are two of the most important prerequisites necessary for the development of reading skills.

60. A: A words correct per minute screening test is used primarily to identify students who have weak reading fluency skills. Reading fluency is the ability to decode words easily, and strong fluency allows students to focus on comprehending the text as a whole.

61. C: The best approach for addressing this concern would be to teach and practice new vocabulary words and concepts prior to beginning the novel. This approach allows the students to become familiar with the vocabulary of the novel before reading it so that they will be able to focus on higher-order skills.

62. D: The most appropriate strategy for a class with students who have such diverse ability levels would be to assign students at each reading level different texts that match their skill levels. This

strategy will not only ensure that all students will find the lesson accessible, but also that they are appropriately challenged.

63. B: In order to develop students' reading fluency, teachers should incorporate extensive practice reading aloud into their lessons. Silent reading is unguided, and so it is very easy for students to simply skip over words with which they are unfamiliar and settle for compromised comprehension. In contrast, guided oral reading gives teachers the opportunity to teach new words and assist with decoding, both of which build reading fluency.

64. B: The primary purpose of informal reading inventories such as the BRI, CRI-CFC, QRI-4, and ARI is to conduct preliminary diagnostic screening to help determine students' instructional needs. Reading inventories can help teachers assess different aspects of students' reading ability and plan instruction based on the strengths and weaknesses that are revealed.

65. C: In order for consequences to be effective in managing behavior, they must be consistently and fairly applied. Both negative and positive consequences can be effective in certain situations, and teachers should employ both types when appropriate. More severe consequences do not necessarily correlate with better behavior.

66. A: Introducing the rules at the beginning of the school year, reviewing them periodically, and citing them when applying consequences is the most effective procedure for encouraging students' adherence to classroom rules. This method demonstrates that the teacher values the rules and wants to ensure they are enforced consistently.

67. C: The most important consideration in designing a seating chart is that the teacher can easily monitor all of the students during instruction and from his or her desk. It is also important for safety reasons that there is sufficient space for students and teachers to move freely among the desks, and that the teacher can see the door from his or her desk and the instructional area.

68. B: The major flaw in this set of rules is that they focus on prohibiting negative behaviors, and do not state what positive behaviors the teacher expects. While there are times when negatively stated rules are necessary, positively stated rules are more effective because they focus students on what they *should* be doing rather than on what they *could* but *should not* be doing.

69. D: All of these rules would be effective if included as part of a set of classroom rules. They are neither too general nor too specific, and they are stated positively.

70. C: Insulting or demeaning a student is not an effective way to deal with misbehavior, no matter how severe. This response sets a poor example for other students because the teacher is modeling a behavior that is prohibited in the classroom (insulting others). In order to ensure adherence to rules, the teacher must follow classroom rules and model respect for others.

71. B: Parents should be informed about students' behavior as soon as a pattern of problem behavior emerges. While it is unnecessary to inform parents every single time their child breaks a rule, parents need to be informed if their child is a "problem student." This should be done as soon as possible so that parents can intervene. Teachers should not wait until conferences roll around to deal with the problem. It can also be very helpful to tell parents when students are behaving well because it positively reinforces students' good behavior.

72. D: In order to ensure that students follow classroom procedures, the teacher should review and rehearse procedures intensively at the beginning of the school year and periodically throughout the year. Students, especially middle and high school students, have many procedures to learn for different classes. Students need time and practice to master them. Procedures are critical to effective classroom management, though, and they should not be eliminated or simplified to save time.

73. D: Ideally, all of these and many more procedures will be taught to students at the beginning of the school year. Professionals emphasize that it is critical to spend time explaining and teaching classroom procedures before instruction begins.

74. C: The major benefit of allowing students to participate in the development of classroom rules is that students are more likely to value and adhere to rules that they helped create. When the teacher is well-prepared for this activity, students typically decide on reasonable, effective rules.

75. C: The most important goal in arranging the physical layout of a classroom is ensuring that it promotes student safety and effective monitoring by the teacher. Although there are many important considerations in designing a classroom layout, student safety and monitoring are the most critical.

76. B: A behavior contract should clearly state what behavior is desired and what positive and negative consequences will be applied should the student choose to exhibit or not exhibit the agreed-upon behavior. A behavior contract does not need to be developed concurrently with the student's parents (although this can be helpful). It is helpful to get the student's input when developing the contract.

77. C: The most important first step in delivering differentiated reading instruction is to assess students to determine the range of reading levels that need to be targeted. This will provide the teacher with the preliminary information needed to plan the differentiated instruction and select appropriate materials.

78. D: The most important resource for unit and lesson planning is state and district instructional standards. While other resources can be helpful, it is the teacher's responsibility to ensure that students learn the objectives selected by the teacher's employers.

79. C: When designing a lesson for a given class period the first step should be to determine what the learning objective for the class period will be. While materials and assessment methods are also important considerations in lesson planning, the most important first step is to write a specific, measurable learning objective.

80. D: Task analysis can be a helpful technique when planning lessons for any of these learning objectives. While task analysis is traditionally associated with physical tasks, it is also a helpful strategy when planning step-by-step lessons on intellectual tasks such as solving math problems and comprehending texts.

81. C: A "check for understanding" that Mrs. Frances could conduct would be to ask the entire class to indicate their level of understanding at critical points during the lesson using hand signals. Checks for understanding are used during instructional delivery to determine whether or not students are following the lesson and to maintain student engagement.

82. B: The most important consideration in unit planning is ensuring that the learning objectives within the unit are logically sequenced so that prerequisite skills are taught first. While it is also important for units to be engaging and reflect students' interests, logical sequencing is critical if students are to master the contents of the unit.

83. C: Mr. Bartlett can avoid similar problems in the future by conducting a diagnostic assessment of his students' prerequisite skills before planning future units. This will allow him to reteach any prerequisite skills that students are missing prior to the unit or adjust the unit to suit students' ability levels.

84. D: Teachers are involved in pre-referral assessments and creating and implementing IEPs. Teachers' participation in these activities is critical to their success because teachers know the students well and have the skill set necessary to identify effective measures to help struggling students.

85. A: The teacher should contact the appropriate authorities immediately. All 50 U.S. states legally require professionals who regularly work with children to report signs of abuse or neglect as soon as possible.

86. B: During the IEP creation process it is the general education teacher's responsibility to attend the IEP meeting and offer any helpful information he or she may have. It is the special education teacher's responsibility to write the IEP and get the parents' approval.

87. C: Section 504 is a general law that is designed to protect disabled individuals from discrimination. It protects all disabled students from discrimination, regardless of whether their disability interferes with their learning. IDEA is specifically targeted at children who have disabilities that interfere with their learning. IEPs are only required for students who qualify for protection under IDEA.

88. A: According to the Individuals with Disabilities Education Act (IDEA), students who are diagnosed with learning disabilities must be placed in the least restrictive environment possible. This means they must remain in the general classroom as much as is practicable, and will only go to the resource room for predetermined periods of time based upon their demonstrated needs. The priority is to accommodate students with disabilities in the regular classroom as opposed to isolating them from general education students.

89. D: According to Florida's Mandatory Reporting law, educators are required to report suspected abuse, neglect, and abandonment to the Florida Abuse Hotline as soon as possible.

90. B: When teaching students to use Internet search engines for research, it is most important that students learn how to distinguish reliable, authoritative websites from unreliable ones. This is the most critical skill students need when using the web for research purposes.

91. D: When determining the quality of a web page for research purposes, students should look for several characteristics. The page should have a low proportion of ads (extensive ads indicate that the page is primarily for profit and the quality of the content may not be high). It should also be professional in appearance, up-to-date, and credited to a reliable author.

92. C: Microsoft PowerPoint would be the most appropriate software product for classroom presentations. This product allows students to create and display slides with text, images, charts, and other features.

93. B: When planning lessons, a teacher who values John Dewey's progressive theory of education would be most likely to encourage problem solving and real-life experience as paths to learning. Dewey also advocated cooperation and the fostering of democratic values in the educational environment.

94. C: The most likely cause of the gap between Maricela's ability to read and her comprehension of what she reads is that Maricela lacks the cultural background knowledge and vocabulary to comprehend these texts. Although she has gained a mechanical understanding of English grammar and spelling, she has still not been exposed to many concepts that are necessary for her to comprehend what she reads. Maricela may be able to recognize and sound out words in a story, but she may lack the background knowledge to comprehend what is going on in the story.

95. A: It is true that the range of intelligence among ESOL students is similar to that among native English-speaking students. Although academic performance among ESOL students may be lower, especially if they are placed in general education classes, this is a function of their limited English proficiency, not lower intelligence. While reading English at home and speaking English with fluent parents can be helpful, limiting students to speaking English at home if their parents are not fluent can restrict their exposure to rich vocabulary and ideas. It can also place severe strain on the family.

96. D: The most effective way to improve Jarithza's academic performance would be to adapt certain aspects of the class to meet Jarithza's needs. Helpful adaptations would include giving directions slowly and clearly, using body language and non-text visual aids to convey concepts, and providing extra reading and writing instruction. These techniques will help Jarithza improve her English and succeed in class without lowering expectations for her or placing undue strain on her family.

97. A: In order to meet the needs of ESOL students in mainstream classes, teachers should incorporate elements related to ESOL students' interests and backgrounds into the curriculum so that they feel valued and accepted. All students should be held to high academic standards, and it is important to acknowledge and embrace diversity so that students from all backgrounds feel accepted.

98. A: When teaching students in the mainstream classroom who have no or extremely limited English skills, it is most important to take steps to build their English vocabulary as much and as quickly as possible. This strategy will give students the rudimentary communication skills they need to get by on a daily basis, and will help them connect with the environment around them.

99. B: Mr. Vale can alleviate this problem by looking for bilingual community members who are willing to serve as translators with parental consent. This approach will protect students' and parents' privacy, ensure the integrity of conferences, and assist parents who have limited English proficiency.

100. A: Juanita, an ESOL student who has not been diagnosed with any learning disabilities but struggles academically, is unlikely to be eligible for special education services. Students must be diagnosed with a disability that interferes with their ability to learn in order to be protected by IDEA, and limited English proficiency is not the result of a learning disability.

Practice Test #2

Practice Questions

1. How can a teacher evaluate student mastery of intended learning outcomes over time?
   a. Analyzing classroom and standardized test scores throughout the year
   b. Gauging student understanding during classroom discussion and group projects
   c. Through a combination of student class work, presentations, performance on assignments, test scores, and participation during class time
   d. Meeting with each student on a monthly basis to discuss classroom concepts, allowing the teacher to assess whether or not each one can demonstrate mastery

2. Which choice describes the most effective instructional design for the corresponding activity?
   a. Students are placed into groups of three to work together on the first chemistry experiment of the year. They record findings on a log sheet created by the teacher.
   b. Each student is given ten minutes at the end of class time to review important concepts independently.
   c. Given that a few students performed poorly on the last unit test, the next day's lessons are devoted to reviewing the concepts as a class.
   d. Following a written comprehension quiz, the teacher instructs students to switch papers with a partner to grade them quickly; each student then has time to correct his or her own work before turning it in.

3. Which statement is false?
   a. Before creating lesson plans, a teacher should analyze the curriculum and educational goals of the course being taught
   b. Students often benefit from knowing the intended learning objectives as well as time frames for instruction ahead of time
   c. Teachers should refrain from sharing information about learning goals with students so that they can make their own assumptions and connections
   d. Lesson plans should be flexible so that teachers and students can explore areas of spontaneous interest during class time

4. Which theory would most support the following statement? There are many 'ways of knowing,' all equal to one another: each student will learn in his or her own manner.
   a. Bloom's taxonomy
   b. Situated learning
   c. Problem-based learning
   d. Multiple intelligences

5. Which approach is best for beginning to teach a group of new students?
    a. Rely on age- and grade-appropriate standards to determine the starting point in the curriculum
    b. Review samples of past class work or test scores, if available, in conjunction with teacher-administered assessment to determine a starting point
    c. Talk with students to gauge their intellectual and maturity levels and attempt to "jump-start" them by introducing challenging work immediately
    d. Ask students to list their interests in detail and use the lists to design instruction that will maintain their attention throughout the course

6. Students with high levels of interpersonal intelligence will be more successful when they:
    a. work in groups
    b. work independently
    c. have a choice of assignments
    d. are allowed to complete assignments in a series of short intervals with frequent breaks

7. Which of the following choices is the best use of homework in regular instruction?
    a. A daily review of classroom concepts to keep information fresh for the next day's lessons
    b. A weekly packet that includes both review of concepts as well as opportunities to practice transferring the skills to new situations
    c. Monthly "extension" projects that require students to research and apply skills to topics of their own choosing
    d. Homework should not be used as a major part of instruction, since teachers cannot be present to guide students

8. What was the first major federal law guaranteeing all children aged 5-21 the right to a public education?
    a. IDEA
    b. EHA
    c. FAPE
    d. LRE

9. Aside from test scores, how might a teacher identify patterned gaps in student knowledge or understanding throughout instruction?
    a. Student responses during in-class, verbal comprehension checks
    b. Student engagement and participation during class and group projects
    c. Both A and B
    d. Neither A nor B

10. A student who suffers from problems with executive functioning will most likely struggle in which of the following areas?
    a. Forming social relationships with peers
    b. Completing assignments on time
    c. Developing motor skills
    d. Learning simple tasks

11. What must a teacher do before he or she will be able to evaluate the effectiveness of the instructional design?
    a. Create an outline of class objectives and how each objective will be assessed or measured
    b. Interpret and analyze student performance on each assignment
    c. Request assistance from peers in observing class instruction and giving vital feedback
    d. Determine each student's capacity for learning

12. Which strategy would be least effective in engaging parent involvement in the classroom?
    a. Sending a letter describing volunteer needs, descriptions, parameters, and times specified for volunteer opportunities
    b. Linking certain kinds of parental involvement to specific benefits during parent orientation
    c. Making phone calls or spending time talking with parents informally to build parent-teacher relationships
    d. Holding parent-education workshops so that parents can understand what their children are learning in class and how they can become involved

13. Critical thinking ability is best assessed using:
    a. authentic assessments
    b. written assessments
    c. oral assessments
    d. criterion-referenced assessments

14. Which technique would likely facilitate more effective small-group activities?
    a. When assigning groups, take great care not to place students who are close friends or who do not get along well into the same group
    b. Part of the assignment is to determine group member "roles" so that all group members are aware of their own and others' responsibilities
    c. Keep students assigned to the same group throughout the course unless there are significant problems to establish continuity and development of cooperation
    d. Change group assignments for each activity to facilitate growth and variation in cooperative learning

15. A high-school chemistry teacher is preparing her lesson plans for the next month. The upcoming unit includes a large amount of complex math that will serve as the foundation for future units. Which daily lesson structure is most appropriate?
    a. Teacher-led review of previous day's content, short demonstration/instruction of concepts, break, group practice, students present results of practice and discuss as a class
    b. Video tutorial, short demonstration/instruction of concepts, student-led review of concepts, complete homework for the upcoming evening in-class
    c. Fun group activity involving movement, teacher-led demonstration/instruction of concepts in detailed format, working each problem in a step-by-step manner, student questions
    d. Short lecture on purpose of class instruction, short teacher-led demonstration/instruction, students take turns working examples in front of the class

16. According to the law's procedural safeguards, who can request a due process hearing regarding the identification, evaluation, placement, or provision of education to a child with a disability?
    a. The child's parents
    b. The parents or the school
    c. The parents' attorney
    d. All of the above

17. Select the answer that most truthfully completes the following statement. Classroom rewards and recognition...
    a. should be delivered in frequent but unpredictable patterns so that students are always striving to earn them
    b. should be based on things students can control, such as attitude, effort, or improvement
    must be explained in detailed way before each assignment or task so that students know what they c. are working toward at all times
    d. are often damaging to student morale, especially when individuals do not receive anticipated praise or rewards

18. Which classroom arrangement is most appropriate for young students in Kindergarten or 1st grade?
    a. Child-sized desks and chairs are placed in a neat grid so that the teacher can always see whether or not the students are in place and on task. All personal belongings, supplies and class work are kept inside individual desk cubbies
    b. Lamps, rugs, and cozy pillows create a home-like atmosphere. Artwork and 'found' objects decorate the halls and tables. When group lessons are given, the students simply listen from wherever they are in the classroom
    c. Certain curriculum areas each have a designated classroom space. Seating is provided in each area and is designed to match the nature of the activities present. Whole-class seating is available at long, arced tables in one area of the room
    d. The classroom chairs and desks are arranged in a U shape to promote discussion and collaboration among students. The children alternate between desks and outdoor play

19. Which method is best for connecting students' personal experiences to course concepts?
    a. Each time a new concept is introduced in Social Studies class, students take turns relating a personal anecdote that exemplifies the material
    b. Keep a running list in Algebra class of how concepts are used in various professions
    c. For a year-end Science project, students pick a topic to research. The written report must include a section describing why the topic is of personal importance to the student
    d. In Psychology class, require weekly journal entries in which students draw or write about personal reflections, provided that entries reflect on concepts taught during the week

20. Which of the following instructional media will meet all of a teacher's criteria for a specific lesson by showing motion, reproducing sounds, and allowing student interaction?
    a. Chalkboard or easel
    b. Computer software
    c. Textbook/handouts
    d. Overhead projector

21. Comparing a student's performance on a test to a national average for age/grade level is a(n)...
    a. Norm-referenced test
    b. Criterion-referenced test
    c. Performance-based test
    d. Ipsative measure/test

22. Which statement is most true regarding classroom rules?
    a. Students are most likely to internalize and take responsibility for following rules when they can be involved in creating them
    b. Teachers should make classroom rule lists as detailed and expansive as possible to cover all situations and eliminate any room for confusion
    c. The most important rule in any classroom is based on the concept: When you are unsure of what to do, always ask the teacher before proceeding
    d. Classroom rules should be modified over time to fit the students, scenarios, and needs in the specific class

23. Which statement is false?
    a. Class material should be presented in a logical sequence based on the objectives of the course
    b. Sequence of lessons can have a variety of foundations: time frames, progression of ideas, overview of topics, or building of skills
    c. All components of a lesson sequence must be presented in detail, even if all students have previously demonstrated comprehension
    d. Instruction sequencing can often be shared with students to facilitate understanding

24. All of the following are types of professional development in which teachers should engage consistently EXCEPT:
    a. meeting with students' parents and guardians
    b. participating in mentor-mentee relationships with other teachers
    c. attending school- and district-mandated seminars on teaching strategies and technology use
    d. conducting self-assessments of teaching effectiveness

25. Which choice describes a/the purpose for assessment in the classroom?
    a. To diagnose student learning needs
    b. To evaluate effectiveness of instruction and curriculum
    c. To monitor all students' progress
    d. All of the above

26. Which of the following activities would be most helpful in encouraging students to explore cultural diversity?
    a. Assigning students a project requiring them to research their family backgrounds
    b. Reading about and discussing the contributions of diverse individuals and cultures in class
    c. Watching a movie about the experiences of immigrants in the U.S.
    d. Asking students to write a personal essay describing their family's cultural values and practices

27. Which teaching technique is described by the following statements? The teacher provides motivation, context, and modeling when presenting subject material. Slowly, the teacher reduces guidance and interaction so that the student can become independent with the material.
    a. Metacognition
    b. Scaffolding
    c. Bradley method
    d. SWT

28. Which assistive technology is most appropriate for a student with a voice disorder that interferes with audible speech production?
   a. Speech-to-text computer software
   b. Text-to-speech computer software
   c. Voice recognition computer software
   d. Voice synthesizer computer software

29. A student who is a kinesthetic learner will comprehend concepts best by:
   a. reading and writing about them
   b. listening to the teacher discuss them
   c. engaging in active, hands-on practice with them
   d. discussing them with others

30. Which use of punishment or consequences is most effective?
   a. Adrian was disruptive and not respectful during class lessons and group work despite repeated requests from the teacher to change his behavior. Adrian has to stay after school and clean the blackboards, sharpen pencils, and complete other classroom tasks.
   b. Tamyra is extremely fidgety and cannot sit still during class. Sometimes, she distracts other students. Tamyra's teacher moves her desk into a space at the back of the class, away from the other students.
   c. Barron is caught skipping class. He receives one day of school suspension. Administrators warn him that if he skips class again, he will be suspended for a longer period of time and possibly expelled from school.
   d. Linda and Ellie are found to have cheated on their science quiz by working together when the teacher was not watching. They each would have made an 88%, but their teacher decides to give them each one-half that grade, resulting in a 44%. They must each sit alone during individual work for the remainder of the term.

31. When is it appropriate for a teacher to lower his or her expectation of a student or group of students?
   a. Never. Teachers who hold consistently high expectations for student achievement usually see better results than those who do not.
   b. When the vast majority of the group has demonstrated effort but has either missed the point of an assignment or failed to complete it successfully.
   c. When he or she is teaching students who are disabled or extremely disadvantaged compared to the rest of the group.
   d. Teachers should not operate based on expectations; students are all different and must learn in highly personal ways. The learning process should be a shared discovery, rather than establishing and meeting of expectations.

32. Which of the following professionals is least likely to work directly with high-needs students in the classroom?
   a. Pediatrician
   b. Occupational therapist
   c. Speech-language pathologist
   d. Counselor

33. All students are required to take a graduation exam. Student performance on this exam is measured against a pre-determined set of learning objectives. Those students who pass the test are permitted to graduate. The graduation exam is a:
   a. norm-referenced test
   b. non-standardized test
   c. student performance assessment
   d. criterion-referenced test

34. Which of the following statements is true of a behavior contract?
   a. It must involve the student's parents.
   b. It should clearly state what behavior is desired and what positive and negative consequences will be applied should the student choose to exhibit or not exhibit the agreed-upon behavior.
   c. The most important part of implementing a behavior contract is the discussion and meeting with the student, and follow-up is not always necessary.
   d. It is not helpful for the student to participate in the development of the contract.

35. Which of the following is the most effective way to incorporate a variety of learning styles into instruction?
   a. Allowing students to choose their own form of assessment
   b. Including visual aids and hands-on practice during verbal instruction
   c. Incorporating technology into instruction and assignments
   d. Inserting stretch breaks into lessons

Questions 36 and 37 pertain to the following passage:
   In class this month, students will be studying a variety of particularly complex human anatomy processes. It is important for each student to grasp the placement and functions of various anatomical organs and systems first. These concepts are the foundation for study of more complex processes in later lessons.

36. Which choice provides the best aid for instruction in the classroom?
   a. Assign one body part and function to each student, to be presented to the class one at a time.
   b. Provide a sturdy, clear, color-coded anatomy chart to each student, upon which he or she can place labels and take notes.
   c. Distribute pre-typed lecture notes to students so that they can focus on listening to what the teacher is saying rather than on capturing the notes.
   d. Show a video on the material from reading assignments to help solidify knowledge.

37. How should the teacher use the correct teaching aid from Question 85 for purposes of assessment?
   a. Use a rubric to grade each student's presentation and gauge understanding of the topic.
   b. Check over student progress on anatomy charts as lectures progress to ensure that students have foundations for future lessons.
   c. Monitor student focus, body language, and verbal responses during lecture and discussions.
   d. Ask students to write down major concepts from the video and assigned readings.

38. All of the following statements are true about the evaluation component of a lesson except:
   a. Evaluation may be group-wide instead of individual
   b. Evaluation must occur in some form with every lesson
   c. Evaluation may occur on an on-going basis
   d. Evaluation may occur again; for example, during a unit test

39. A teacher uses a variety of un-graded assignments and quizzes to help guide her instructional decisions through units of instruction. This type of assessment would be described as:
   a. Formative
   b. Summative
   c. Narrative
   d. Diagnostic

40. According to Howard Gardner's theory of multiple intelligences, which of the following statements is true?
   a. Everyone has only one type of intelligence.
   b. Students who don't do well in schools that emphasize linguistic and logical-mathematical intelligence may still be highly intelligent in other domains.
   c. Schools often overwhelm students by asking them to activate too many different types of intelligence at once.
   d. Students who have high levels of musical, physical, or interpersonal intelligence usually perform poorly in school.

41. Which of the following tasks would be most appropriate for a child at the concrete operational stage of cognitive development?
   a. Grouping objects into categories by shape and color
   b. Solving a word problem using algebra
   c. Identifying the main idea of a story
   d. Grasping and stacking blocks

42. During which step of the IEP process are classroom accommodations and modifications tested for effectiveness?
   a. Identification
   b. Pre-referral
   c. Eligibility
   d. Review

43. The type of assessment most often used to evaluate the effectiveness of instruction is a(n)...
   a. Authentic assessment
   b. Ongoing assessment
   c. Formative assessment
   d. Summative assessment

44. Which of the following is most congruent with general ethical principles regarding assessment information?
   a. Informally disclosing student test results to members of school faculty or staff
   b. Breaking confidentiality in cases of obvious danger to an individual or to society
   c. Making formal reports of students' assessment results before parent consent
   d. Assessing culturally diverse students regardless of lack of cultural competence

45. Which of the following strategies would be most likely to encourage students' intrinsic motivation to learn?
    a. Designing lessons that incorporate students' personal experiences and interests
    b. Providing positive reinforcement for students' effort, as well as for achievement
    c. Offering prizes such as candy and free time to the highest-performing students
    d. Posting the work of high-performing students in a public place in the classroom as an example

46. Which of the following is the most important consideration when designing a seating chart?
    a. Students like and feel comfortable with the students sitting near them.
    b. Students can easily turn their desks to work in groups.
    c. The teacher can easily monitor all of the students during instruction and from his or her desk.
    d. The teacher's desk is in a convenient location near the instructional focal point of the room.

47. Which of the following teacher behaviors demonstrates application of the principles of mastery learning?
    a. Grading student work on a "curve"
    b. Allowing all students to pursue independent study and conduct self-assessments of their progress, regardless of their current academic levels
    c. Requiring students to demonstrate competence in prerequisite skills before allowing them to proceed to subsequent lessons
    d. Dividing students into groups based on academic performance and assigning them more or less challenging assignments accordingly

48. Which of the following is an independent federal agency that makes recommendations to both the President and Congress regarding issues related to disabilities?
    a. Federation for Children with Special Needs (FCSN)
    b. Center for Personal Assistance Services (CPAS)
    c. National Disability Rights Network (NDRN)
    d. The National Council on Disability (NCD)

49. According to Bloom's taxonomy of cognitive skills, which of the following activities requires the highest-order cognitive thinking skills?
    a. Memorizing a list of foreign-language words and their English equivalents
    b. Creating an invention for the school science fair
    c. Applying a newly-learned geometry formula to solve a story problem
    d. Reading and understanding the contents of an academic paper

50. Which of the following is the most effective procedure for encouraging students' adherence to classroom rules?
    a. Introducing the rules at the beginning of the school year, reviewing them periodically, and citing them when applying consequences
    b. Developing a complex list of potential negative behaviors and their consequences, and requiring students and their parents to sign a copy
    c. Allowing students to decide on and enforce classroom rules democratically
    d. Passing out a copy of the classroom rules and procedures and requiring students to keep it with them at all times

51. What kind of assessment instrument is most likely to show a normal distribution?
    a. A criterion-referenced measure
    b. A norm-referenced instrument
    c. A performance-based measure
    d. A portfolio assessment measure

52. Relative to public schools, the basic legal and ethical principles on which both FERPA and the student record Privacy Rule of HIPAA were founded…
    a. Are completely unrelated
    b. Overlap in some areas
    c. Are the same principles
    d. Differ in important ways

53. Which of the following statements do NOT typically describe students with emotional disabilities?
    a. They may exhibit inappropriate social behaviors
    b. They experience frequent episodes of anxiety and depression
    c. Their emotional disability may cause them to struggle academically
    d. They have unusually high self-esteem

54. The most important goal in arranging the physical layout of a classroom is:
    a. ensuring that the colors of displays are well-coordinated and relevant to lessons
    b. leaving space open to display student work
    c. ensuring the layout of the room promotes student safety and effective monitoring by the teacher
    d. ensuring that the teacher can move easily around the room during lessons

55. An anticipatory set is used by teachers to:
    a. provide additional practice for students who have not yet mastered a learning objective
    b. focus students on the upcoming lesson and tap into prerequisite knowledge
    c. teach prerequisite skills
    d. do none of the above

56. According to the Code of Ethics and Principles of Professional Conduct of the Education Profession, which of the following is NOT an obligation of professional educators?
    a. Making a reasonable effort to protect students from conditions harmful to learning
    b. Maintaining the confidentiality of personally identifiable information
    c. Ensuring that students have a safe home environment
    d. Making a reasonable effort to protect students from harassment and discrimination

57. Which statement is false?
    a. Assessment should be ongoing and provide information that spans a period of time, rather than isolated or discreet points in time
    b. Educators should use educational values and objectives as the foundations for assessment design
    c. The most effective assessments are observational and personal in nature; descriptions should be recorded by an educator who knows the student well
    d. Assessments should be used to monitor patterns in student and teacher performance

58. Which classroom arrangement is most appropriate for a high school Civics class?
    a. Desks and chairs are arranged into rows. Posters are hung on the walls outlining fundamental important classroom concepts. All chairs face the front of the room, where the teacher lectures
    b. The arrangement changes based on the type of class structure for the week. For lectures and class discussion, students sit in a circle. For small group work, students sit in small groups. At times, the floor may be cleared for activities or audiovisual displays
    c. Students sit on comfortable chairs and couches during class. The teacher moves around the room to engage the students in lecture, discussion, or activities
    d. The class is arranged into learning stations. Students move through the stations during self-directed class time and are able to work with partners if they so choose

59. According to Madeline Hunter's "Instructional Theory into Practice" teaching model, which of the following is the best example of guided practice?
    a. Students complete an assignment in pairs
    b. A teacher works one-on-one with a student to help him or her complete an assignment
    c. Students practice a skill they have just learned and receive immediate feedback from their instructor
    d. The teacher completes problems on the board while the students take notes

60. The cognitive state of children between the ages of two and six who are at the preoperational stage according to Piaget's Stages of Cognitive Development can be best characterized as:
    a. benevolent
    b. egocentric
    c. abstract
    d. logical

61. The most important FIRST step in delivering differentiated reading instruction is to:
    a. select materials for different reading levels
    b. design differentiated assessments appropriate for students at varied reading levels
    c. assess students to determine the range of reading levels that need to be targeted
    d. place students in reading groups based on their overall academic performance

62. In order to ensure that students follow classroom procedures, the teacher should:
    a. minimize the number and complexity of procedures as much as possible
    b. give students written instructions for all procedures
    c. apply severe consequences when students forget procedures
    d. review and rehearse procedures intensively at the beginning of the school year and periodically throughout the year

63. Which of the following is the best example of a specific, measurable learning objective?
    a. The student will be able to identify the parts of a cell
    b. The student will understand the causes of the Civil War
    c. Students will know about electricity
    d. Students will learn about the Great Depression

64. According to Piaget's Stages of Cognitive Development, children are best equipped to engage in problem solving and critical thinking at the:
    a. concrete operational stage
    b. preoperational stage
    c. formal operational stage
    d. sensorimotor stage

65. In regard to the process of writing a lesson plan, which of the following is true?
    a. The steps of writing the plan may vary with the teaching model
    b. Experienced teachers won't need to write down as much as new teachers because some actions become automatic with time
    c. The lesson's opening, body, and closing should be written in order
    d. Only the parts of the lesson to be presented to the students need to be written down, not necessarily the pre-planning and editing tasks

66. The major benefit of allowing students to participate in the development of classroom rules is that:
    a. it is a fun activity that helps students feel comfortable in the classroom
    b. it makes it easier for students to remember the rules
    c. students are more likely to value and adhere to rules they helped create
    d. this activity teaches students about democratic processes

67. The most important resource for unit and lesson planning is:
    a. student textbooks
    b. the students' own interests
    c. Internet resources and academic journal articles
    d. state and district instructional standards

68. Which of the following actions would constitute a violation of the Code of Ethics and Principles of Professional Conduct of the Education Profession?
    a. Intentionally making false statements about a colleague
    b. Misrepresenting one's professional qualifications
    c. Interfering with a colleague's ability to exercise their political or civil rights
    d. All of the above

69. For teachers to be comfortable with student diversity and to help students to be comfortable with diversity, teachers should:
    a. Review the stereotypes they have learned and find ways to bring reality to these views
    b. Study the cultures they encounter among their students
    c. Encourage students and parents to share about their cultures
    d. All of the above

70. Mr. Jones has strong suspicions that a student is being physically abused at home. The student has not confirmed that abuse has occurred, but the student's physical condition suggests that this is the case. How should the teacher proceed?
    a. He should contact the appropriate authorities immediately
    b. He should not take any action unless the student admits that abuse has occurred
    c. He should not say anything since it is not his business
    d. He should schedule a conference with the parents to confront them

71. When designing a lesson for a given class period, which of the following steps should be completed FIRST?
    a. Selecting the reading or stimulus material that the students will use
    b. Choosing an assessment method for the material to be learned
    c. Determining what the learning objective for the class period will be
    d. Considering what instructional materials are available

72. Tanya is an 11th grade student who has been legally adopted by her aunt and uncle. She is under 18 years of age. The Family Educational Rights and Privacy Act (FERPA) states that a school would need to obtain her guardians' permission to release Tanya's educational records in all of the following situations EXCEPT when:
    a. a local organization is evaluating students for college scholarships and wants Tanya's transcripts
    b. Tanya's mother calls the school to find out how she is performing in her classes
    c. Tanya is transferring to another school and the new school needs her records
    d. the agency that helped with Tanya's adoption requests a copy of her grades

73. Of the following, which is often the resolution to parent/teacher cultural conflicts?
    a. The conflict is resolved through compromise; i.e., both teacher and parents making accommodations
    b. The conflict is resolved when the teacher changes her actions to address the parents' concerns
    c. The conflict is resolved through parent education about American cultural practices
    d. The conflict is not resolved and parents/teacher continue their own practices

74. Which one of the following statements about objectives is not true?
    a. An objective describes a learning outcome
    b. An objective describes where we want students to go
    c. An objective describes how to get to the outcome
    d. An objective describes the lesson focus and direction

75. Task analysis can be a helpful technique when planning lessons for which of the following learning objectives?
    a. The student will be able to solve a two-step algebraic equation
    b. The student will be able to tie his or her shoes
    c. The student will be able to find the main idea of a news article
    d. All of the above

76. Julio is a high school student, and his parents have called the school to express their dissatisfaction with his grade in science. They and Julio believe that he was unfairly penalized for missing a test due to illness, and that this significantly lowered his overall grade for the course. The school has determined that the teacher did penalize Julio in accordance with his own and the school's policies. The school has therefore refused to change Julio's grade. The Family Educational Rights and Privacy Act (FERPA) states that since Julio's parents' request has been denied, Julio's parents are entitled to:
    a. request a formal hearing on the school's decision
    b. insert a note into Julio's file that documents their dispute regarding the grade
    c. request that the teacher be suspended
    d. do none of the above; FERPA does not grant them the right to take any further action

77. The emotional balance of a classroom can be upset by conflict. Appropriate methods for a teacher to use in handling conflict do not include:
   a. Gathering information and re-capping the situation
   b. Allowing children to come up with a solution themselves
   c. Letting the issue drop once a solution has been agreed upon
   d. Dealing with the conflict calmly and with a quiet voice

78. Effective management of children with behavioral problems would include:
   a. Preparing explicit instructions
   b. Following up instructions with focused, active practice
   c. Giving immediate feedback
   d. All of the above

79. Which of the following is the most important consideration for unit planning?
   a. Ensuring the unit has a fun and engaging theme
   b. Ensuring the learning objectives within the unit are logically sequenced so that prerequisite skills are taught first
   c. Ensuring students' interests and experiences are incorporated into the unit's theme
   d. Ensuring critical thinking skills are integrated into the unit

80. Which of the following actions would constitute a violation of the statute of the Code of Ethics and Principles of Professional Conduct of the Education Profession that prohibits giving or receiving gifts in exchange for favors?
   a. Rewarding students who perform well on standardized tests with a pizza party
   b. Giving candy and other small prizes to students who are well-behaved
   c. Helping a neighbor with yard work in exchange for a free laptop computer for the classroom
   d. Taking money from a student's parents in exchange for tutoring that student during the teacher's prep period

81. During a lesson, which of the following is the best method for classroom management?
   a. Making rewards contingent on everyone doing well
   b. Promising a treat for good work to be given at the end of the week
   c. Communicating behavioral expectations clearly before the lesson starts
   d. Customizing the consequences for misbehavior to fit each student

82. Considerations for additional behavior management include all but which one of the following:
   a. Re-arranging seats to ensure compatibility and avoid conflict
   b. The teacher rather than the students selecting partners
   c. On-the-spot corrections since you can't plan ahead for what might happen
   d. Stronger reinforcements to keep students on task

83. Teachers are involved in which of the following activities for at-risk students?
   a. Implementing pre-referral interventions
   b. Creating Individualized Education Plans (IEPs)
   c. Implementing IEPs and evaluating their effectiveness
   d. All of the above

84. According to the Code of Ethics and Principles of Professional Conduct of the Education Profession, a licensed educator must report arrests or charges involving possession of a controlled substance or abuse of a child within:
    a. 2 hours
    b. 24 hours
    c. 36 hours
    d. 48 hours

85. In order to make the best use of time and avoid lags in time that would allow student restlessness, a teacher should NOT:
    a. Check out equipment to make sure it is working before the lesson
    b. Rely on standard clean-up rules to take care of the close of the lesson
    c. Clearly announce rules for sharing and returning supplies before the activity starts
    d. Have supplies or handouts ready for distribution

86. The best approach to using technology in the classroom is:
    a. Expect to teach technology with your subject
    b. Rely on the school's technology center rather than your own classroom
    c. Use only the technology with which you are comfortable
    d. Increasing technology will improve instruction

87. Which of the following is a general education classroom teacher's responsibility during the IEP creation process?
    a. Convening the IEP conference
    b. Attending the IEP conference
    c. Writing the IEP
    d. Getting the student's parents to approve the IEP

88. In order for consequences to be effective in managing behavior, they must be:
    a. uniformly negative
    b. uniformly positive
    c. consistently and fairly applied
    d. sufficiently severe to act as a deterrent

89. Which of the following statements is true?
    a. Students who write compositions using the computer often take more pride in their work than those who use pen and paper
    b. Spell check allows student to focus on content and not mechanics
    c. Computers allow for almost effortless reorganizing and thus less time and energy
    d. All of the above

90. Which of the following should not be a consideration about using computers in the classroom?
    a. Does the state test allow for writing on computers?
    b. Is the software easy to use and fun?
    c. Will I have sufficient technical back up if anything goes wrong?
    d. Will behavior management be more difficult while students are on computers?

91. The following statements deal with the availability of computers in the classroom. Which statement is false.
    a. Numerous federal and state grants have enabled high poverty and minority schools to catch up to high socio-economic schools in number of students per computer
    b. Only one or two computers available in your classroom may limit use to demonstrations and word processing
    c. More than two computers in a classroom adds the possibility of doing collaboratives, independent research, portfolios, and research papers
    d. Only about 30% or fewer students will have computers at home unless the family income is $50,000 per year or more

92. Which of the following is NOT an effective way to deal with a student who has repeatedly broken classroom rules?
    a. Moving that student to a desk away from other students
    b. Sending that student to a "time out" in another classroom
    c. Insulting or demeaning the student
    d. Creating a behavior contract with the student

93. Which of the following students is most likely NOT eligible for special education services?
    a. Juanita, an ESOL student who has not been diagnosed with any learning disabilities but struggles academically
    b. Victor, who has a cognitive impairment caused by a mild brain injury
    c. Sylvia, who has been diagnosed with ADHD
    d. All of these students would be eligible for special education services

94. In order to meet the needs of ESOL students in mainstream classes, teachers should:
    a. incorporate elements related to ESOL students' interests and backgrounds into the curriculum so that they feel valued and accepted
    b. never openly acknowledge any differences between ESOL students and students who are native English speakers
    c. hold ESOL students to lower academic standards than other students
    d. sacrifice the academic needs of students who are proficient in English in order to focus on ESOL students

95. Which of the following statements about Section 504 of the Americans with Disabilities Act and the Individuals with Disabilities Education Act (IDEA) is correct?
    a. Students who qualify for Section 504 protection always qualify for protection under IDEA.
    b. Both IDEA and Section 504 only provide protection for students who have a disability that interferes with their learning.
    c. IDEA contains procedural safeguards for students with disabilities that interfere with their learning, while Section 504 is designed to protect all disabled individuals from discrimination.
    d. Both students who qualify for protection under IDEA and those who qualify for protection under Section 504 must receive Individualized Education Plans (IEPs).

96. Which graphic organizer would be most helpful for practice with comparison and contrasting of ideas or objects?
    a. SQ3R chart
    b. Venn diagram
    c. Flower diagram for the "5 W's"
    d. Bar graph

97. When planning lessons, a teacher who incorporates John Dewey's progressive theory of education would be most likely to:
    a. teach students who are struggling separately from the rest of the class
    b. encourage problem solving and real-life experience as paths to learning
    c. provide material rewards for excellent academic performance
    d. encourage competition among students as a means of motivation

98. When teaching students to use Internet search engines for research, it is most important for the teacher to design a lesson that covers:
    a. how to use search operators such as site: and loc:
    b. how to distinguish reliable, authoritative websites from unreliable ones
    c. how to download and use antivirus software
    d. how to build websites

99. According to the Individuals with Disabilities Education Act (IDEA), students who are diagnosed with learning disabilities must be placed in the:
    a. least restrictive environment possible
    b. safest environment possible
    c. environment in which they will be least disruptive
    d. most beneficial environment possible

100. Parents should be informed about students' behavior:
    a. only when it is negative
    b. as soon as a pattern of problem behavior emerges
    c. every time a student breaks a classroom rule
    d. only at parent teacher conferences

Answers and Explanations

1. **C:** Students demonstrate mastery over a period of time. True mastery is the ability to understand and apply knowledge in various circumstances over the course of time (rather than on just one occasion). By changing circumstances and increasing length of time for demonstration of mastery, teachers can ensure that the student has retained knowledge in long-term memory and understands it well enough to use it in a variety of contexts. Therefore, the teacher will need to look at a variety of contexts when determining student mastery. Some students do well on tests but have trouble during class discussions, or vice versa. Often, a student will retain knowledge for a short period of time and not be able to recall it. By using a varied approach to student assessment, the teacher will gain a better understanding of what each student has mastered.

2. **A:** Once a teacher has determined what learning outcomes are intended, he or she must design instruction to facilitate those specific outcomes. There are times when certain types of instruction will be more effective than others; also, introducing variety in instructional design will help maintain student interest and engagement. It is likely that students will need some guidance and help when they do anything for the first time, especially something as complex as a science experiment. By placing students into small groups, the teacher will facilitate cooperative learning and peer guidance, thus allowing her more time and freedom to help students who need it.

3. **C:** It is usually beneficial for teachers to share information about what concepts students will learn in class. Depending on the age and abilities of the students, it may even be helpful to provide a timeline of concepts and assignments in the form of a syllabus. By sharing this information with students, they can understand the purpose behind what they are learning, thus increasing personal responsibility in the learning process. Students can also use these shared learning goals to evaluate their own understanding whenever needed. Once all topics are covered, the teacher may also choose to use the conceptual framework and timeline as a tool for review.

4. **D:** Howard Gardner first introduced the concept of multiple intelligences. His theory rests on the idea that there are multiple ways to understand or 'to know.' Every individual will have strengths and weaknesses in learning, but everyone will learn in different ways. The seven commonly identified intelligences are: verbal/linguistic, existential, logical/mathematical, interpersonal, intrapersonal, visual/spatial, musical/rhythmic, bodily/kinesthetic, and naturalist.

5. **B:** When teaching a new group of students, the teacher must design instruction that will be at an appropriate level of challenge. If course work is too easy or too challenging, the students may lose confidence and interest early on. If samples of past work or performance on tests are available, the teacher should review these whenever possible. Doing so will give him or her insight into the students' past instruction and abilities. However, the teacher should also be sure to provide a current assessment of some type to account for changes in classroom environment and knowledge retention. The teacher should ensure that students meet objectives for the end of the term or course, but will need to begin at an ability-appropriate level for the students.

6. **A:** Students with high levels of interpersonal intelligence may benefit most from working in groups. This is because they are adept at and enjoy interacting with others. In contrast, students

with low levels of interpersonal intelligence may perform poorly when asked to work in groups because their social skills are not as well-developed.

7. B: Homework can function as an important extension of classroom instruction. Ideally, students will learn the process of taking responsibility for their own learning and will recognize the importance of continuing the learning process outside the classroom. Teachers are present to instruct and guide during class, but students can and should review concepts outside class to transfer them to long-term memory. Students also have the opportunity to apply both old and new knowledge to new situations outside class, or during homework. The best type of homework includes both review and opportunities for transfer of knowledge.

8. B: The Education for all Handicapped Children, or Education for the Handicapped Act (EHA) was passed in 1975 (Public Law #94-142) to guarantee everyone with disabilities aged 5-21 a Free Appropriate Public Education/FAPE (C). It stated that all students with disabilities must be educated as much as possible in the Least Restrictive Environment/LRE (D). In 1990, this law was reauthorized and renamed the Individuals with Disabilities Education Act/IDEA (A). It was later amended in successive reauthorizations in 1991, 1997, and 2004.

9. A: Teachers should regularly work to identify patterns of understanding of course material (or lack thereof). However, formal testing is usually not frequent enough to serve as the only form of assessment. Waiting until test time minimizes a teacher's chances to re-present or clarify concepts. Introducing in-class "comprehension checks" will allow the teacher to evaluate student understanding without taking time away from instruction; additionally, the teacher will also be able to modify instruction immediately to increase understanding. Participation or engagement does not always signify understanding, especially if the topic presented is interesting for students.

10. B: A student who suffers from problems with executive functioning will most likely struggle with completing assignments on time. Executive functioning disabilities such as ADHD make it difficult for individuals to concentrate on tasks for a prolonged period of time. Students with such disabilities may need to be seated away from other students to avoid distractions, and they may need to complete assignments in intervals with short activity breaks in between.

11. A: Maintaining a framework for class objectives is very important before planning or evaluating effectiveness of lessons. The teacher must determine first what concepts need to be addressed during the course. He will then need to create corresponding measures of assessment for these objectives. In other words, he will decide ahead of time how to measure whether or not his objectives are being achieved. Once the objectives and assessment techniques have been created, the teacher can refer to them when he wants to analyze whether or not the method of instruction is functioning effectively.

12. A: Many parents want to be involved in their child's education, or at the very least are open to the notion that becoming involved will benefit their child. However, most parents do not have the educational expertise or flexibility of schedule that allows them to be at school during the day. Setting up strict parameters about involvement is more likely to discourage parents from being involved. However, building personal relationships, explaining the benefits of involvement, and being flexible about scheduling is more likely to encourage involvement. The more parents know about what is happening in class, the more likely they will be to identify ways in which they can help.

13. A: Critical thinking ability is best measured using authentic assessments. Since a student's ability to solve problems is a reflection of critical thinking ability, it is crucial that critical thinking skills be tested with authentic problems for which the student has not already been given a solution. For instance, solving a math problem when the teacher has just modeled how to solve that type of problem several times does not require critical thinking skills. Instead, students are simply applying a rote formula. However, solving a word problem that does not directly state what needs to be calculated does require critical thinking skills.

14. B: Group-based activities are beneficial for inspiring creative thinking, cooperative learning and student engagement. However, students must learn how to work effectively in groups over time. The teacher in this scenario requires students to determine specific roles within the group. This requirement will cut down on confusion in the early stages of the activity as students try to agree on who will be responsible for what tasks. Students may also experience less frustration since every individual will have responsibility (preventing some students from getting credit for minimal participation). Not only will the group work be more accurate and efficient, but students will achieve the indirect aim of the assignment, which is to strengthen their abilities to cooperate with one another.

15. A: Detailed curriculum can be challenging to teach effectively, given multiple barriers to student learning: focus and engagement can diminish with long periods of complex instruction. The lesson plan described includes a variety of contexts in which students can internalize the concepts. The teacher includes review of concepts to help increase retention each day, as well as a short presentation of the day's concepts. Giving the students a break will allow them to take care of personal needs and refocus their energy in class. Group practice will allow students to understand the concepts through doing, rather than listening, and will encourage peer feedback and assistance. Finally, the class discussion will correct any mistakes and serve as an interim review for the day.

16. D: Under the 2004 amendments to the IDEA, procedural safeguards state that a due process hearing can be requested not only by the child's parents (A), not only by the parents or school (B), and not only by the parents' attorney (C), but by the parents, the school/public agency, or their attorneys.

17. B: Rewards and recognition can be useful tools in education, but should not be the sole focus of each activity. Growth and learning should be the primary goals of any assignment. However, most students respond positively to recognition of their work. If teachers focus on positive, controllable aspects of student work, those students will be more likely to understand that effort, attitude, consistency, and other traits are beneficial in the learning process. This model also allows teachers to recognize all students, rather than limiting rewards to students who achieve correct or positive results on the first attempt. The recognition in choice B focuses on actions that will help the students in the long-term and can be applied without discrimination.

18. C: Young children at a Kindergarten or 1st-grade level are still learning to sit still, read and write fluently, and increase attention spans. For these reasons, the classroom environment should provide a variety of activities and seating spaces. Certain activities require certain body positions; for instance, when writing, students should be seated at a desk of the appropriate height, but for a group lesson or discussion, students might be able to sit in a circle on the floor. In this choice, each activity determines the type of seating and space allotted, increasing likelihood that students will achieve the intended learning outcomes.

19. D: All students will relate personal experience to course objectives in different ways. In fact, some students may not instinctively apply personal knowledge to what they are learning unless encouraged to do so frequently. By keeping a personal journal, students can thoroughly explore what they have learned in class, as well as ideas or experiences that can be connected to that content. Students will be more likely to feel comfortable expressing personal concepts if the forum is private (a journal that will only be seen by the teacher and student) and if the format is flexible (being able to draw or write).

20. B: Computer software meets all of the listed criteria. A chalkboard or easel (A) allows student interaction but does not meet the other requirements. Textbooks and handouts (C) do not fulfill any of the criteria, though they have many other desirable characteristics (portability, allowing highlighting/writing/drawing in or on them, availability after the lesson, independent use, etc.). Overhead projector (D) presentations (and Power Point® or other computer presentations) allow writing/highlighting/drawing, let students control the pace, are easily modified, etc., but they do not meet these other specific criteria either.

21. A: Norm-referenced tests compare the student's score to norms, such as national averages of scores for students of the same age or grade level. These are standardized tests, such as national achievement tests including the SAT, ACT, GRE, etc. Criterion-referenced tests (B) do not compare students' scores to other students' scores, but rather measure students' performance against a criterion, standard, or objective previously determined and given to students before testing. Class quizzes, exams, oral reports, presentations, experiments, and performance-based tests (C) are examples of criterion-referenced tests. Ipsative measures or tests (D) compare the student's performance to his/her own previous performance.

22. A: Classroom rules are important and necessary. Whenever a group of individuals must share a space and resources while working toward a common goal, there will be conflicts or difficult circumstances. Rules are helpful in creating norms amongst any social group and will help ease anxiety in uncomfortable situations. However, members of any group are most likely to abide by the rules if they can participate in creating them; when students have a say in what rules are appropriate, they will probably take more ownership over time. Students will feel as though their feelings and needs have been addressed, or in the least 'heard,' and assist in enforcing rules in class.

23. C: Teachers must not only plan instructional content, but the sequence of instruction as well. This sequencing can be found in various formats, as long as the presentation is logical and can be explained easily to another person. However, if students show that they understand a concept fully, there is no need to present it as such during class. It is important to resist the urge to teach curriculum simply because it has been outlined and planned ahead of time. Presenting previously mastered material would waste valuable teaching time and would fail to further student progress.

24. A: Teachers should engage in all of these activities consistently, but meeting with students' parents and guardians is a community outreach activity as opposed to a professional development one. Professional development activities such as attending training, collaborating with peers, and engaging in self-assessment are all pursuits that help teachers improve their professional practice through reflection and learning. Conferencing with students' parents and guardians is an aspect of professional practice that can be improved through development activities.

25. D: Assessment is a vital component of both teaching and learning. All curriculum design must begin with establishment of goals and objectives. Assessment allows educators to determine how well these goals have been met. The purpose of assessing student progress serves a variety of

functions in addition to providing grades. Teachers can identify any gaps in student learning; make decisions about future instruction; assess original goals; and more. Assessments can also be used to evaluate teachers' performance and identify professional development goals.

26. B: Reading about and discussing the contributions of diverse individuals and cultures in class would be most helpful in encouraging students to explore cultural diversity. This activity allows students to learn about and discuss cultures other than their own as opposed to actively or passively reflecting on their own experiences.

27. B: Scaffolding is a technique intended to provide diverse methods of instruction for students and gradual withdrawal of teacher assistance. In the initial phases of scaffolding, the teacher guides students on class concepts or activities. He or she helps motivate and instruct the students, often modeling problem-solving, ideas and steps. Over time, the teacher reduces involvement in dealing with the concepts so that students can become more independent in the learning process.

28. D: Computer software with a voice synthesizer produces a digital voice for those who cannot speak. Speech-to-text software (A) allows a person to speak into a computer microphone and the program produces typed text of the spoken language. This helps those who can speak but cannot write or type. Text-to-speech software (B) also produces a synthesized voice to read text, but these programs typically scan the text and read it aloud to assist those with visual impairments and reading difficulties, not to supply a substitute speaking voice. Voice recognition software (C) also transcribes spoken language into typed text, similar to the closed-captioning feature on televisions.

29. C: A student who is a kinesthetic learner will comprehend concepts best by engaging in active, hands-on practice. Auditory learners learn best by listening, and visual learners comprehend concepts by watching the teacher model tasks and looking at visual aids.

30. D: All students must learn over time that there are consequences for their actions. However, it is important not to shame or unduly criticize students for their behavior, since they are still growing and learning what behaviors are acceptable. Linda and Ellie's teacher chose a consequence that was directly related to their inappropriate action: since they worked together, they each got half the grade. The consequence for cheating was to fail the exam, but the teacher made a point about their behavior with the way she chose to handle the situation. The teacher also prevented the same scenario from happening again by assigning different seats for the girls for future individual work.

31. B: All students have different capabilities and capacities for learning. But teachers should not be in the habit of raising and lowering expectations for individuals based on these factors; doing so would unnecessarily limit or put pressure on individual students. There may be times when teachers must *change* individual expectations for students or assignments, but disadvantage or disability does not mean that students can never achieve intended learning outcomes. Each class activity must have intended learning goals and/or purposes in order to have meaning and create growth. In rare occasions, most of the group will try to complete an activity and fail to do so. The teacher should use these instances to examine his or her own expectations for reasonability and efficacy, and change or lower them accordingly. However, teacher expectations for student *capacity* should not change; he or she should maintain high expectations for all students.

32. A: Countless kinds of professionals are available to work with students in the classroom, including: occupational therapists, speech and language pathologists, counselors, paraprofessionals, and specialized therapists for specific disorders. Procedures for classroom interventions will vary by school and system; however, most classrooms now hold some children who are differently-abled

or who have special needs. This change means that outside professionals will often work with students in class. However, pediatricians are not typically found in classrooms. These doctors are usually involved in the educational process for specific patients, but are not the experts most qualified to work with students on a day to day basis in the classroom.

33. D: Students are often required to take a variety of exams as the progress through school; most students will have some form of standardized testing during this time. Criterion-referenced tests are based on a pre-determined set of concepts or objectives. Test questions are organized around these concepts and student performance should indicate individual levels of mastery. By contrast, norm-referenced tests measure student performance by comparing student scores to other student scores; the measure of competency is based on comparison to other students, rather than to pre-determined objectives.

34. B: A behavior contract should clearly state what behavior is desired and what positive and negative consequences will be applied should the student choose to exhibit or not exhibit the agreed-upon behavior. A behavior contract does not need to be developed concurrently with the student's parents (although this can be helpful). It is helpful to get the student's input when developing the contract.

35. B: Including visual aids and hands-on practice during verbal instruction will expand the appeal of a lesson to visual and kinesthetic learners, as well as auditory learners. While technology can *help* teachers appeal to students with a variety of different learning styles, simply incorporating technology will not necessarily be enough.

36. B: The initial information describes lesson content as complex and detailed; students must understand a large quantity of information in a relatively short period of time in order to progress in class. Concepts can be classified in many ways, and in this case, should be considered "spatial." Human anatomy is spatial in nature, meaning that students can process information based on how concepts relate to one another in space. Since students will be learning first about parts of the body and their functions, it makes sense to provide students with a spatial aid to help them understand where the parts are located. The spatial representation of the body will also help students understand how systems and organs are related to one another. Re-creating images of the body would be time-consuming, so the teacher has provided the charts such that students can focus on labeling and annotating rather than drawing.

37. B: The anatomy charts are visual and spatial; therefore, they provide a quick method of assessing how well students have understood material. The teacher can easily look over students' charts throughout lecture and group work to ensure that no one has missed vital information or incorrectly annotated the charts. If need be, charts can be turned in and then checked after class. Since the information presented is vital to the next phase of instruction, the teacher has a vested interest in making sure that students have the best tools possible.

38. A: The teacher needs to know how well each student is doing and must teach each child. The teacher is striving for a quality learning experience for every child rather than averages or high percentages measured by a group-wide evaluation. It is true that evaluation must be part of every lesson, in some form or another, or else the teacher will not know if the objective was reached, and if some or all students need a re-teach. This evaluation can continue with retention checks in other lessons; that is, on an on-going basis, and may be repeated in overall unit tests.

39. A: Formative assessment is typically used during the process of instruction. Formative evaluations allow teachers to gauge student progress for purposes of monitoring and modifying instruction. These assignments are usually not graded, although at times there may be exceptions to this rule. Summative assessment is used at the end of a grading term or instructional unit to provide a summary of how well a student grasped and retained concepts.

40. B: According to Howard Gardner's theory of multiple intelligences, students who don't do well in schools that emphasize linguistic and logical-mathematical intelligence may still be highly intelligent in other domains. Gardner theorizes that there are eight domains of intelligence, many of which are not emphasized in traditional educational environments. As a result, students who are highly intelligent in these areas may be mistakenly classified as underachievers.

41. C: Identifying the main idea of a story would be most appropriate for a child at the concrete operational stage of cognitive development. Children at this stage are developing the capability of induction (generalizing from a specific instance), but have not yet developed the capacity for deductive logic that is required for abstract thinking.

42. B: The pre-referral stage of the IEP process includes interventions and other activities in the general education classroom to screen students before any formal referral is made for special education. Testing classroom accommodations and modifications for effectiveness is one of these activities. If accommodations, validated teaching methods, instructional modifications, consultation and help from specialists do not remedy learning problems, the next step is referral. After that, identification (A) is made and eligibility (C) is determined for special education services. Review (D) of the IEP is made after it has been implemented to evaluate progress and, if necessary, change the IEP.

43. D: Summative assessments are given after instruction, such as tests at the ends of chapters, units, semesters, or terms; school district interim assessments or benchmark assessments; standardized state tests, etc. As such, they are often used to evaluate the effectiveness of instruction. Authentic assessments (A) are made in real-life situations, such as driver's license tests, or in simulations of real life. Ongoing assessments (B) are like formative assessments (C) in that they are made during instruction rather than after it. Formative assessments can be equated with practice that students receive as part of instruction, rather than scoring or grading what has already been learned as summative assessments do.

44. B: It is congruent with general ethical principles maintained by most professional organizations that, when there is clear and present danger to an individual or to society, an assessor should break confidentiality regarding assessment results. Ethical principles dictate that assessors should not informally disclose student test results to other school employees (A). It is also considered unethical to report students' assessment results formally before obtaining their parents' consent (C) if they are minors (or the student's consent if the student is not a minor). Ethical principles additionally require that an assessor avoid assessing culturally diverse students if that assessor does not demonstrate the cultural competence to do so because assessing them regardless (D) would be inappropriate.

45. A: Designing lessons that incorporate students' personal experiences and interests would be most likely to encourage students' intrinsic motivation to learn. Intrinsic motivation stems from a personal desire to acquire knowledge for its own sake rather than as a means to external rewards such as status or prizes.

46. C: The most important consideration in designing a seating chart is that the teacher can easily monitor all of the students during instruction and from his or her desk. It is also important for safety reasons that there is sufficient space for students and teachers to move freely among the desks, and that the teacher can see the door from his or her desk and the instructional area.

47. C: Requiring students to demonstrate competence in prerequisite skills before allowing them to proceed to subsequent lessons is one of the fundamental principles of mastery learning. Proponents of this approach argue that the vast majority of students can grasp all academic concepts taught if they are given sufficient time and quality instruction.

48. D: The National Council on Disability is an independent federal agency that makes recommendations to the President and Congress regarding issues related to disabilities. The FCSN (A) is an organization founded in Boston, Massachusetts that informs, helps, and supports parents of children with disabilities, involved professionals, and communities. The CPAS (B), formed by the University of California, San Francisco (UCSF) through a grant from the National Institute on Disability and Rehabilitation Research (NIDRR), supplies research, dissemination, training, and technical help with personal assistance services concerns nationwide. The NRDN (C) represents the needs of its members in Protection and Advocacy (P&A) before federal agencies and Congress, but is not itself a federal agency and does not make recommendations to the president.

49. B: According to Bloom's taxonomy of cognitive skills, creating an invention for the school science fair requires the highest-order cognitive activity because it involves synthesis, evaluation, and creation. According to Bloom's original taxonomy, evaluation is the highest-level cognitive task, followed by synthesis. In the revised taxonomy by Anderson, creation is the highest-level task, followed by evaluation.

50. A: Introducing the rules at the beginning of the school year, reviewing them periodically, and citing them when applying consequences is the most effective procedure for encouraging students' adherence to classroom rules. This method demonstrates that the teacher values the rules and wants to ensure they are enforced consistently.

51. B: Norm-referenced tests compare individual student scores to national averages. With the majority of school populations taking these standardized tests, plotting their scores will yield a normal distribution, or "bell curve," where the majority had average scores and minorities had higher- and lower-than-average scores. Criterion-referenced measures (A) measure individual students' results against a criterion previously established by the teacher, school, or district but do not compare them, so there would be no distribution. As criterion-referenced measures, performance-based assessments (C) would also not show a distribution. Portfolio assessments (D) are made by teachers of individual students' portfolios of work produced over time. These typically are not meant to be compared with other students' work, so there is no statistical distribution.

52. C: The Family Education Rights and Privacy Act (FERPA) and the Privacy Rule for student health records of the Health Insurance Portability and Accountability Act (HIPAA) are founded on the same basic legal and ethical principles. FERPA is designed to protect confidential information in students' school records pertaining to education, and HIPAA is designed to protect any confidential health information that is individually identifiable, including student health records in public schools or in any schools covered by FERPA.

53. D: Students with emotional disabilities may exhibit inappropriate behaviors in social settings, experience academic difficulties, and struggle with anxiety and depression that impede their

normal academic and social functioning. Although a small minority of students with emotional disabilities may exhibit high self-esteem, the vast majority of such students experience social rejection and have low self-esteem.

54. C: The most important goal in arranging the physical layout of a classroom is ensuring that it promotes student safety and effective monitoring by the teacher. Although there are many important considerations in designing a classroom layout, student safety and monitoring are the most critical.

55. B: An anticipatory set is used to focus students on the upcoming lesson and tap into prerequisite knowledge. Anticipatory sets can take the form of brief writing assignments or activities that mentally prepare students for the upcoming lesson by activating relevant prior knowledge.

56. C: Ensuring that students have a safe home environment is not an obligation of professional educators. However, educators are required by state and federal law to report suspected neglect, abuse, or abandonment to the proper authorities.

57. C: There are countless forms of assessment: formal and informal, graded and un-graded, observational and standardized. Educators should utilize a variety of formats to evaluate student needs and progress, rather than focusing on one method. While observational assessment can be very beneficial in some cases, all students should be given a variety of assignments/tests to measure and describe their learning experiences. Each type of assessment provides different kinds of insight into the complex processes that take place in education.

58. B: No singular classroom arrangement is likely to be appropriate for the whole of a class term. The best classroom instruction is based on purposeful instruction and variety to keep students engaged. In choice B, the classroom is set up to facilitate the type of activity going on that week. Changing the type of instruction and the physical space will prevent classes from becoming boring and predictable. Students are more likely to stay focused and interested if they are learning in different ways over time. This approach also allows the teacher to cater to various learning styles (visual, kinesthetic, auditory).

59. C: According to Madeline Hunter's Instructional Theory into Practice teaching model, an example of guided practice would be students practicing a skill they just learned and receiving immediate feedback from their instructor. Guided practice occurs immediately after direct instruction (when the teacher introduces the learning objective) and checks for understanding (when the teacher interacts with students to informally confirm they understand the new material).

60. B: The cognitive state of children between the ages of two and six who are at the preoperational stage according to Piaget's Stages of Cognitive Development can be best characterized as egocentric. Children at this stage of cognitive development are not typically capable of the type of abstract thought required to truly understand and consider another person's point of view.

61. C: The most important first step in delivering differentiated reading instruction is to assess students to determine the range of reading levels that need to be targeted. This will provide the teacher with the preliminary information needed to plan the differentiated instruction and select appropriate materials.

62. D: In order to ensure that students follow classroom procedures, the teacher should review and rehearse procedures intensively at the beginning of the school year and periodically throughout the

year. Students, especially middle and high school students, have many procedures to learn for different classes. Students need time and practice to master them. Procedures are critical to effective classroom management, though, and they should not be eliminated or simplified to save time.

63. A: "The student will be able to identify the parts of a cell" is an example of a learning objective that is both specific in terms of the task that the student is expected to be able to perform and measurable in the sense that the teacher can concretely observe the extent to which the student is able to perform the task.

64. C: According to Piaget's Stages of Cognitive Development, children are best equipped to engage in problem solving and critical thinking at the formal operational stage. This stage begins around age 12, and is marked by the emergence of abstract logic.

65. B: The lesson plans for an experienced teacher do not have to be as detailed as they should be for a new teacher because some actions become second nature to a teacher after a while and go without saying. The steps to writing a good lesson plan do not vary with the teaching model but are the backbone of every lesson. The lesson opening, body, and closing do not need to be written in order; in fact, it is often best to write the body of the lesson first so that the teacher has had a chance to thoroughly think through the lesson before deciding on an appropriate opening. Since the lesson plan has a set pattern, all parts must be written, including pre-planning steps and editing tasks, not just the parts that will be presented to the students.

66. C: The major benefit of allowing students to participate in the development of classroom rules is that students are more likely to value and adhere to rules that they helped create. When the teacher is well-prepared for this activity, students typically decide on reasonable, effective rules.

67. D: The most important resource for unit and lesson planning is state and district instructional standards. While other resources can be helpful, it is the teacher's responsibility to ensure that students learn the objectives selected by the teacher's employers.

68. D: Intentionally making false statements about a colleague, misrepresenting one's professional qualifications, and interfering with a colleague's ability to exercise their political or civil rights all constitute violations of the *Code of Ethics and Principles of Professional Conduct of the Education Profession*.

69. D: All the answers are linked by the teacher's need to know more about the students' cultures. Inadequate knowledge that might lead to a misunderstanding with a student or parent needs remediation, first through recognition of any gaps of knowledge and then by various means of getting to know the cultures. Most people's knowledge about other cultures contains some stereotypes. For teachers who have a multi-cultural classroom, it would be beneficial for them to think through what they know about the cultures of the children in their classrooms to analyze whether any of that knowledge is based on stereotypes. They need to question themselves as to whether they have any first-hand knowledge about these cultures. If not, they need to devote a little time to studying about these cultures. One way to learn is to ask the children and their parents to share information about their cultures for the benefit of all.

70. A: The teacher should contact the appropriate authorities immediately. All 50 U.S. states legally require professionals who regularly work with children to report signs of abuse or neglect as soon as possible.

71. C: When designing a lesson for a given class period the first step should be to determine what the learning objective for the class period will be. While materials and assessment methods are also important considerations in lesson planning, the most important first step is to write a specific, measurable learning objective.

72. C: The Family Educational Rights and Privacy Act (FERPA) states that a school would need to obtain Tanya's guardians' permission to release her educational records to her mother (who is not her legal guardian) or to outside organizations. However, Tanya's school would not need permission to send Tanya's records to her new school.

73. D: Unfortunately, it is fairly common that no one tries to resolve the problem. Through fear of speaking up or ignorance of the problem, the situation continues and irritates all concerned. There are a variety of ways to solve a conflict. One is through mutual compromise; another is for one side to change. In the case of a parent/teacher cultural conflict, there could be give-and-take on both sides, or the teacher could adjust to the cultural needs of the family, or, when the demands of the classroom cannot accommodate the cultural demands, the parents can be helped to come to an understanding of the requirements through education.

74. C: The teacher is trying to communicate to the students what the learning outcome is, not how to get there. The lesson itself provides the "how." An objective is defined as a clearly described learning outcome so that students know what they are expected to learn. It is an outline of where the teacher wants the students to go in their learning that day in class. Writing an objective on the board gives the lesson focus and direction that also helps in the selection of appropriate practice activities and evaluations.

75. D: Task analysis can be a helpful technique when planning lessons for any of these learning objectives. While task analysis is traditionally associated with physical tasks, it is also a helpful strategy when planning step-by-step lessons on intellectual tasks such as solving math problems and comprehending texts.

76. A: The Family Educational Rights and Privacy Act (FERPA) states that since Julio's parents' initial request was denied, they have the right to a formal hearing. If the hearing does not result in a decision by the school to amend the record, then Julio's parents would be entitled to insert a note into Julio's file that documents their dispute regarding the grade.

77. B: There should be follow-up to the conflict resolution to make certain that the children are sticking to their agreed-upon solution and to ensure that the conflict does not re-occur. Some teachers might feel that dropping the issue will help everyone forget the conflict, but that usually is not the case. Conflicts are best handled with calmness and a quiet voice as the teacher gathers information about the conflict in order to get a complete and fair picture of the situation. Then the teacher should review the conflict with the children and ask for their ideas for ways the problem could have been prevented and ways to solve the conflict. Involving the children in the resolution of the problem teaches them self-regulation and respect for themselves and others.

78. D: All of the responses demonstrate that clear and immediate communication is the best way to deal with children with behavioral problems. Children with behavioral problems are best managed with clear, distinct communication. Therefore, potentially vague instructions must be revised prior to presentation to be as explicit as possible so the child cannot claim to have misunderstood or argue that the teacher said something else. This type of students does best when there is not a gap

of time between instructions and practice, but rather by immediate involvement in the activity while the child still remembers what to do and has not yet had a chance to get distracted. The same sense of immediacy is needed for feedback or the student will not be able to connect the feedback to the activity.

79. B: The most important consideration in unit planning is ensuring that the learning objectives within the unit are logically sequenced so that prerequisite skills are taught first. While it is also important for units to be engaging and reflect students' interests, logical sequencing is critical if students are to master the contents of the unit.

80. D: Taking money from a student's parents in exchange for tutoring that student during the teacher's prep period would constitute a violation of the statute of the *Code of Ethics and Principles of Professional Conduct of the Education Profession* that prohibits giving or receiving gifts in exchange for favors. In this case, the gift is causing the teacher to pay undue attention to a particular student rather than helping students as equitably as possible.

81. C: Clear communication is always best for effective classroom management, especially when instructions and expectations are delineated before the lesson starts. Saying that a reward will be given "if everyone does well" is too vague and sets up conflicts. Rewards, like assessments, should be dependent on individual effort, generally. Younger children do not usually have the focus or sense of time to be able to wait for an award for a week, or to associate an award with the action that earned the reward over a week's time. Awards should be given as close to the lesson or activity for which the reward was offered as possible. "Customizing" consequences for misbehavior would be exhausting for the teacher, confusing for the children, and at risk of being interpreted as favoritism or discrimination.

82. C: The teacher should anticipate problems and be prepared with appropriate reactions rather than trying to think of what to do on the spot. Teachers need to be flexible, and unexpected things will happen, but the wise teacher will try to anticipate behavioral problems that might result from a changed situation. Stepping outside the classroom routine for special activities can result in chaos unless the teacher anticipates problems and plans for additional behavior management specific to the new situation. This planning should include how to re-arrange the seats so that the activity can proceed with sufficient space and accommodate groups or partners if needed; selecting the partners so that teams work well together; and reinforcing the rules with strong reminders of consequences.

83. D: Teachers are involved in pre-referral assessments and creating and implementing IEPs. Teachers' participation in these activities is critical to their success because teachers know the students well and have the skill set necessary to identify effective measures to help struggling students.

84. D: According to the *Code of Ethics and Principles of Professional Conduct of the Education Profession*, a licensed educator must report arrests or charges involving possession of a controlled substance or abuse of a child within 48 hours. In addition, teachers must "self-report any conviction, finding of guilt, withholding of adjudication, commitment to a pretrial diversion program, or entering of a plea of guilty or Nolo Contendre for any criminal offense other than a minor traffic violation within forty-eight (48) hours after the final judgment."

85. B: The routine clean-up process may not be sufficient if extra materials or messy substances such as glue or paint have been used. Effective time management would include anticipation of the

need for additional clean-up instruction and time; otherwise, students might rush or leave a mess when the routine proves insufficient for the task. Teachers shouldn't assume that the students know what to do for clean up when the situation changes. Total preparation means checking out the equipment prior to classroom use to avoid problems, having all the supplies ready so there are no delays while supplies are hunted for or pulled out of cabinets, and giving lesson-specific instructions about sharing and returning materials prior to students jumping into the lesson so that the activity does not have to be interrupted for corrective instruction or additional information.

86. C: The best approach for a teacher in regards to using technology in the classroom is to use only the technology with which s/he is comfortable so that the technology does not complicate or distract from the lesson. Answer A is not the best approach because while the teacher should know enough to demonstrate the technology used in the classroom, it is not the teacher's job to teach technology; therefore, the teacher should not be hesitant to use technology out of fear of having to become a technical expert. Answer B is not the best approach because the teacher needs to find a balance between using the technology center and working with computers in the classroom. It is more convenient to stay in the classroom, but the technology center exists to expand capabilities. Answer D is not the best approach because while increasing technology might improve instruction, there is no guarantee; only better teaching can improve instruction.

87. B: During the IEP creation process it is the general education teacher's responsibility to attend the IEP meeting and offer any helpful information he or she may have. It is the special education teacher's responsibility to write the IEP and get the parents' approval.

88. C: In order for consequences to be effective in managing behavior, they must be consistently and fairly applied. Both negative and positive consequences can be effective in certain situations, and teachers should employ both types when appropriate. More severe consequences do not necessarily correlate with better behavior.

89. D: The answer is all of the above because all of the statements about the benefits of student computer use for compositions are true. Answer A is true because students do not have to worry about penmanship and neatness when writing on a computer, so they find the product more attractive and likely to get a better grade. Answer B is true because the students don't have to worry about their spelling, or grammar for that matter, if they use the spelling and grammar checks. This means that they can relax and concentrate on the content itself. Answer C is true because the cut-and-paste feature of the word processor allows for easy reorganizing and rewriting, which saves time and energy.

90. A: The research shows that instruction and student progress are greatly aided by the use of computers. Some states actually forbid the use of computers in certain areas because computers can't be used on the state test, but this prohibition ignores the benefits of computer instruction and the ability of students to transition to testing without computers. Many teachers have serious trepidations about using computers in the classroom. When trying to figure out whether they can handle the technology or whether there will be sufficient benefit from using computers, teachers should ask if the software is complicated and boring or easy to use and fun for the students. Teachers should also ask whether there will be sufficient technological support if anything should go wrong. If the teacher is software and hardware with insufficient technical support, h/she runs the risk of having the software running on only a few computers, or multiple computers not working properly. Teachers should be concerned about the effect of computers on student behavior; on this issue they should be reassured that student behavior is generally better when students, who love technology, can be engaged by a computer.

91. A: Despite the large number of federal and state grants to help schools with high poverty and minority populations to catch up with schools in higher socio-economic areas, the poorer schools still lag behind in technology. Answer B is a true statement about the limitations placed on the teacher and students if there are not enough computers available for use in the classroom; not much more can be done than demonstrations and the occasional individual work. Answer C is true in that having more than two computers in the classroom allows more student access for collaboratives; allows more time on computers for students since they don't have to share as much; and enables students to work on more complex projects, such as research and portfolios. Answer D is true and very important to know; while we assume that all kids are fans of technology, that does not mean that they have access to technology at home, and the income level for having a home computer is perhaps surprisingly high.

92. C: Insulting or demeaning a student is not an effective way to deal with misbehavior, no matter how severe. This response sets a poor example for other students because the teacher is modeling a behavior that is prohibited in the classroom (insulting others). In order to ensure adherence to rules, the teacher must follow classroom rules and model respect for others.

93. A: Juanita, an ESOL student who has not been diagnosed with any learning disabilities but struggles academically, is unlikely to be eligible for special education services. Students must be diagnosed with a disability that interferes with their ability to learn in order to be protected by IDEA, and limited English proficiency is not the result of a learning disability.

94. A: In order to meet the needs of ESOL students in mainstream classes, teachers should incorporate elements related to ESOL students' interests and backgrounds into the curriculum so that they feel valued and accepted. All students should be held to high academic standards, and it is important to acknowledge and embrace diversity so that students from all backgrounds feel accepted.

95. C: Section 504 is a general law that is designed to protect disabled individuals from discrimination. It protects all disabled students from discrimination, regardless of whether their disability interferes with their learning. IDEA is specifically targeted at children who have disabilities that interfere with their learning. IEPs are only required for students who qualify for protection under IDEA.

96. B: Graphic organizers and visual displays are vital to reaching all types of learners. Each student learns differently and some concepts are easier to understand when using two-dimensional organizers. Venn diagrams consist of two overlapping ovals or circles, creating three separate spaces for students to record ideas. The outer areas can be used to identify differences in objects or ideas; the overlapping area is intended for their similarities.

97. B: When planning lessons, a teacher who values John Dewey's progressive theory of education would be most likely to encourage problem solving and real-life experience as paths to learning. Dewey also advocated cooperation and the fostering of democratic values in the educational environment.

98. B: When teaching students to use Internet search engines for research, it is most important that students learn how to distinguish reliable, authoritative websites from unreliable ones. This is the most critical skill students need when using the web for research purposes.

99. A: According to the Individuals with Disabilities Education Act (IDEA), students who are diagnosed with learning disabilities must be placed in the least restrictive environment possible. This means they must remain in the general classroom as much as is practicable, and will only go to the resource room for predetermined periods of time based upon their demonstrated needs. The priority is to accommodate students with disabilities in the regular classroom as opposed to isolating them from general education students.

100. B: Parents should be informed about students' behavior as soon as a pattern of problem behavior emerges. While it is unnecessary to inform parents every single time their child breaks a rule, parents need to be informed if their child is a "problem student." This should be done as soon as possible so that parents can intervene. Teachers should not wait until conferences roll around to deal with the problem. It can also be very helpful to tell parents when students are behaving well because it positively reinforces students' good behavior.